Business Guides on the Go

"Business Guides on the Go" presents cutting-edge insights from practice on particular topics within the fields of business, management, and finance. Written by practitioners and experts in a concise and accessible form the series provides professionals with a general understanding and a first practical approach to latest developments in business strategy, leadership, operations, HR management, innovation and technology management, marketing or digitalization. Students of business administration or management will also benefit from these practical guides for their future occupation/careers.

These Guides suit the needs of today's fast reader.

Andrea Montua

Guiding Transformation

Empowerment with Strong Leadership and Clear Communication

 Springer

Andrea Montua
MontuaPartner Communications GmbH
Hamburg, Germany

ISSN 2731-4758   ISSN 2731-4766   (electronic)
Business Guides on the Go
ISBN 978-3-658-49754-5   ISBN 978-3-658-49755-2   (eBook)
https://doi.org/10.1007/978-3-658-49755-2

Preface

Dear reader,

Change can be great—when it gets warmer outside, we move into a different apartment, or we meet new and exciting people. And also when we change ourselves, take up new hobbies, or develop further in our families, circles of friends, and organizations. This rarely makes us feel uncomfortable. Change itself is no reason for that.

Or do you get nervous when you look out of a train window and watch the ever-changing landscape fly by as you travel from the north to the south of your country? Probably not.

Right now, the waves of change are hitting some of us particularly hard. Geopolitically, there seem to be few signs of calm, the economy is giving people headaches in many industries, and there appears to be no long-term relief in sight.

For those of us who are responsible for communication, and in this context also for culture within an organization, one thing is clear: change is and will remain part of our daily work. The good news is that we can prepare ourselves excellently for this if we keep one thing in mind:

Transformation begins with people—and above all with ourselves. It's not a one-time goal but a living process. Properly planned and implemented, it strengthens us and our organizations, and makes us fit for the future.

Why This Book?

In our daily work, we see that transformations are reaching a new level, a new quality. Compared to the change processes in recent years, there are now additional aspects that are intensifying the drama: on the one hand, change is taking place on many levels, with processes running simultaneously or overlapping. We see the economic and geopolitical situation as unpredictable, and developments in the field of artificial intelligence are also fueling fears. It's a challenging mix.

With this book, we want to show what it takes to successfully shape change and emerge from it stronger. To this end, we take a brief look at the needs of employees, managers, and how processes can help to meet these needs.

Corporate culture is at the heart of every successful transformation because it shapes the thoughts, feelings, and actions of everyone involved—both visibly and invisibly. It affects everything: how we deal with uncertainty, the quality of communication, the courage to innovate, and whether change is merely endured or actively shaped.

And we look to you, dear reader, who are steering and accompanying this change. As a manager, communications or HR professional, organizational developer, or change manager, you're at the interface between information transfer and responsibility for what employees know and think and how they feel. Your job is not only to explain change, but to make it truly tangible so that employees feel valued and included and the change is ultimately successful.

And that's where this book comes in—with practical, immediately actionable approaches for your daily work. We'll show you how to:

1. ... communicate transformation in a way that employees understand so that they see the meaning behind the change.
2. ... actively live leadership in change by providing guidance and building trust.
3. ... use narratives and storytelling in a targeted way to make complex topics graspable.

4. ... maintain motivation and commitment, even when the pressure to change increases.
5. ... make results visible to embed success and make changes sustainable.

The Greatest Stress, the Greatest Opportunity

When approached correctly, transformative processes offer enormous opportunities. And they can be enjoyable. We put in place new structures, develop corporate cultures, and strengthen teams. These are all tasks that are worth doing—with enthusiasm and a positive attitude.

With this book, we want to help you recognize all these opportunities and take advantage of them. If you'd like more information on topics relating to internal communications, we recommend our book "Führungsaufgabe Interne Kommunikation—Erfolgreich in Unternehmen kommunizieren—im Alltag und in Veränderungsprozessen" (Internal Communications as a Management Task—Communicating Successfully in Companies—in Everyday Life and Change Processes). It's published in German by Springer Gabler.

I look forward to meeting you soon at a conference or hearing from you via LinkedIn or e-mail so we can exchange experiences about the current transformations.

All the best to you and your change processes.

Andrea Montua

P.S. There's a microsite for this book (German only) where you can find helpful checklists, case studies, and tips for your transformation: https://montua-partner.de/essentials

Hamburg, Germany   Andrea Montua

What You'll Find Essential Here

- **Practical methods and tools for sustainable change:** Communication and leadership are fundamental components of successful transformation. In this book, we present a range of tools, including communication formats, leadership approaches, and techniques for dealing with resistance. You'll receive immediately actionable ideas for your own transformation projects.
- **Focus on people as a factor for success:** We show how culture, communication, and leadership can be actively used to drive change, anchor it sustainably, and involve managers and employees in the process.
- **Practical examples and best practices:** Examples from everyday business life illustrate how other transformation-related processes have been successfully managed—and what mistakes can be avoided.

Contents

About the Author

Andrea Montua runs MontuaPartner Communications, a **strategy consultancy for transformation, culture, and communication** in the DACH region. Since 2004, she and her team have been advising and supporting corporations, medium-sized (family-owned) companies, and public sector authorities during phases of change.

This includes the further development of leadership and corporate culture as well as the establishing, enhancing, and professionalizing of internal communications within companies. The goal is to bring organizations (back) to their human strengths, increase the resilience of companies when it comes to change, and intensify employee engagement and loyalty.

In her podcast "Auf einen Tee" (Over a Cup of Tea), Andrea Montua talks to experts from various fields to shed light on relevant topics from the everyday work of communications managers and executives. Her book "Führungsaufgabe Interne Kommunikation: Erfolgreich in Unternehmen kommunizieren—im Alltag und in Veränderungsprozessen" (Internal Communication as a Management Task: Communicating Successfully in Companies—in Everyday Life and Change Processes) was published in its second edition in spring 2024, also by Springer Gabler Verlag.

This book was also written with the valuable and indispensable collaboration of **Christiane Capps**. Christiane has been an editor for internal and external communications for more than 25 years and joined the MontuaPartner Communications team in 2020. She supports clients and the internal team in writing stories of change and accompanying employees on their journeys through processes of change.

Lastly, ChatGPT helped to refine and organize the text and providing us with inspiration during the writing process.

List of Figures

1

What Makes Transformation Successful

Three key points:

1. **Change isn't the same as transformation:**
   Not all change is the same. While change processes tend to optimize structures and processes and remain within the project environment, transformations go to the heart of the matter. They change organizations at their core—including their cultures and identities, and the attitudes of those working within them.
2. **No clarity without a story:**
   Transformation requires more than just information; it needs stories that connect people. A strong vision, honest dialogue, and emotion-oriented communication create the foundations on which employees can build. Those who merely make announcements will move nothing and no one.
3. **Culture beats strategy:**
   Technologies and processes can always be changed or introduced. However, whether transformation is truly successful depends on existing culture. To change culture, creating visions, defining values,

© The Author(s), under exclusive license to Springer Fachmedien
Wiesbaden GmbH, part of Springer Nature 2025
A. Montua, *Guiding Transformation*, Business Guides on the Go,
https://doi.org/10.1007/978-3-658-49755-2_1

making leadership tangible, and enabling communication "at eye level" are just some of the issues that are critical to success.

1.1 Transformation and Change: Why Change Isn't Always Change

Every project, every concept, every topic we tackle in our daily work is usually based on analyzing current challenges and circumstances. This is also the case with change processes. However, we are observing an unfortunate trend here: the conflating of two different topics, namely change and transformation.

Example

Anna M. has been with a company for 10 years and knows the industry inside out. Her mechanical engineering company is famed for its quality and reliability. But the world is changing. Sustainability, digitalization, and increasing competitive pressure are forcing the long-established company to act. As head of corporate strategy, she faces a daunting challenge: production must become more resource-efficient and more networked. New automation software has already been introduced—but the hoped-for change has not materialized.

Her biggest challenges:

- The workforce is skeptical about the changes—many fear for their jobs.
- The corporate culture is focused on stability, not innovation.
- Managers are clinging to old structures and implementing changes only half-heartedly. Agile working methods aren't being explored.

Anna realizes that more than just a new system is needed. A change in culture and mindset is required among employees. A transformation. It's clearly not enough just to change tools and processes when the mindset within the company is focused on maintaining the status quo. New ways of working and thinking, new roles, and different kinds of decision-making are needed. But how can she achieve this?

Definition

In today's business world, companies are constantly faced with change. But not all change is the same—the terms "change" and "transformation" are often used synonymously, but they are fundamentally different:

- **Change** is an adjustment within an existing culture and existing structures. Processes, tools, or strategies change, but the basic framework remains the same. For example, new software may be being introduced, and processes are continually being optimized.
- **Transformation** goes deeper. It changes not only the "how" but also the "why," the "what," and often the "who." It involves a fundamental change in the culture and identity of a company—for example, when a traditional industrial company evolves into a digitalized service provider.

Communication works differently in both cases:

- **Change communication** requires clear implementation plans, communication of milestones and results, quick responses, and strong expectation management.
- **Transformation communication** needs to take people on a journey, convey meaning, and take fears seriously. It calls for much more dialogue, more emotionally intelligent approaches, and a longer-term perspective.

Important

Companies often believe they are initiating a change process, when in fact it is more of a profound, transformative change. The result: misunderstanding and frustration among the people who are supposed to bring the change to life—employees and managers. And, ultimately, failure. Because transformation is not the same as change; it can't be achieved "just like that." Employees have different questions, different fears, and different needs when change affects the entire organization, including working methods and existing patterns of thinking.

1.2   Challenges and Stumbling Blocks in Transformation

Transformation-oriented projects often fail due to stumbling blocks that companies can identify and avoid at an early stage. One of the biggest hurdles is a lack of (or poor) communication. If employees don't understand why a change is necessary, where the pressure is coming from, and what the vision behind it is, uncertainty and resistance arise. Take Anna from our example: the introduction of new software, which on closer inspection turned out to be more of a fundamental change in the way people work together. If this process is treated just as an unexplained change, failure is inevitable. Without a long-term vision, employees might feel ignored or threatened, reject the new solution, and/or may even actively boycott it.

Role models in an organization are equally important. Managers, for example, must actively exemplify the changes. If management strives for an innovative corporate culture but at the same time adheres to rigid decision-making processes and seemingly countless approval stages, employees lose confidence in the change. Credibility is created when the management team leads by example and embraces change itself.

Change often fails because too many projects are being put into practice at the same time. If a company introduces new machines, launches agile methods, and undertakes comprehensive restructuring all at once, the result is overload. Prioritizing key areas and formulating the big picture (see Chap. 6 helps companies achieve sustainable success, never losing sight of the overall goal.

1.3   Curves, Formulas, and Models that Guide us through Change

Change processes entail changing the communication needs among employees and managers. One model for explaining why energy for or against change can be positive or corrosive and inhibiting is the change formula proposed by Beckhard and Harris (1977):

$$C = L \times V \times K > W$$

This equation describes the conditions for successful transformation:

C (change): Energy arises when the following factors are sufficiently high:

- **L (level of dissatisfaction)**: Dissatisfaction with the current situation must be great enough for change to be viewed as necessary.
- **V (vision)**: A clear, attractive vision of the future is needed to provide orientation and inspire people.
- **K (tangible steps)**: Change requires a well-thought-out, realistic plan with measurable stages.
- **W (resistance/costs)**: The perceived costs of change (e.g., effort, uncertainty, loss of routines) shouldn't exceed the energy for change.

If one of these factors is missing or too weak, change will be slow or will fail. Without vision, transformation remains disoriented, and without tangible steps, it remains stuck in theory.

But this is not the only pitfall. Change rarely happens in isolation; rather, numerous change processes take place simultaneously in most companies. One project is not yet finished while the next one is already beginning. This is where managers and communications come in, keeping track of everything and, above all, keeping employees informed.

Streich's (2016) classic scheme of change describes the following (emotional) phases of change (see Fig. 1.1):

1. Phase: Shock—people are overwhelmed and reject the change on an emotional level— feelings such as anxiety and worry characterize the situation—productivity declines.
2. Phase: Rejection—the change is recognized and rejected on the basis of rational reasons.
3. Phase: Rational insight—people realize that the planned changes are unavoidable and start to consider their usefulness.
4. Phase: Emotional acceptance—after rational consideration initially signaled willingness, emotions now follow (the "valley of tears")— inner rejection disappears and new types of behavior emerge.
5. Phase: Learning—people begin not only to let the change happen but also to actively shape it and learn from it.

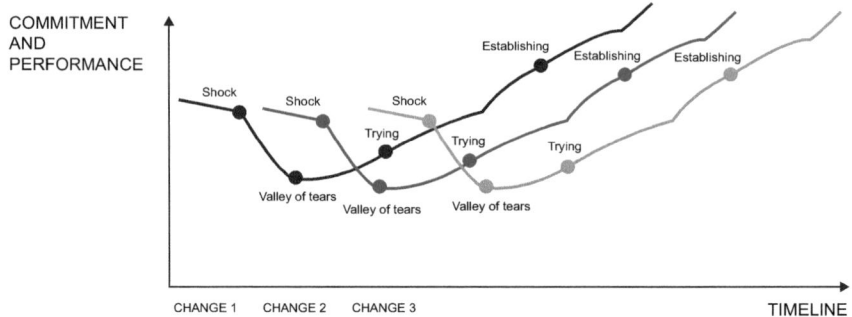

Fig. 1.1 Based on the seven phases of change according to Richard K. Streich (source: author's own representation)

6. Phase: Realization—employees experience positive aspects of the change and begin to like it—curiosity then makes way for positive evaluation.
7. Phase: Integration—new workflows and processes are firmly integrated into people's day-to-day working lives, resulting in an increase in performance.

In everyday life, change processes rarely occur in isolation; the curves overlap. For communication, this means that:

- **Synchronization is essential:** Change communication needs to position the new in an understandable overall context (the "big picture"; see Chap. 6).
- **Different target groups, diverse needs:** Communication must therefore be tailored to the specific target group.
- **Coherent core messages:** Even if different changes are taking place, an overarching vision should be recognizable.

When it comes to the question of "how," communications managers can draw inspiration from **John P. Kotter's 8-step model** (Kotter, 1996). Although it dates to the 1990s, it has lost none of its relevance and shows that sustainable change doesn't just happen by chance—it has to be consciously managed. These are the steps:

- Create urgency
- Build a strong leadership team
- Develop a clear vision
- Communicate the vision
- Eliminate obstacles
- Achieve short-term successes
- Continue to drive change forward
- Embed the change in the culture

1.4 Thinking about Change Holistically: A Systemic View of Transformation

A systemic view of change is always helpful, and this is even more true when the change is more of a transformation (see Sect. 1.1). If change isn't really taking off despite new working groups, efficient project plans, and redefined Key Performance Indicators (KPI), it may be because your organization isn't made up of machines but is a living, social system. Companies can't be managed in a linear way; they evolve through the interaction of people, patterns, expectations, and informal rules.

If we reduce transformations purely to "change management," we won't do justice to the topic and success might not be achieved. A new organizational chart, an agile framework, or a fresh leadership model won't change a system. The question isn't only: What do we need to do? The questions are: What's keeping the old system in place? And: What would need to happen to make the new system not only possible but also attractive?

The Power of Systemic Interactions: How Unrecognized Dynamics Hinder Transformation—And how to Make Them Visible
Systemic thinking focuses on connections: changes in one area have an impact in completely different fields. These interactions are often underestimated—or not even noticed. For example, a company decides to shift decision-making authority to its teams, but at the same time maintains centralized reporting requirements and budget approvals. The result: the

system contradicts itself. New roles remain vacant, old patterns continue to dominate—and managers come under pressure to justify themselves.

System-focused—or systemic—analysis can help to reveal these tensions. Tools such as stakeholder mapping, systemic structural constellations, or working with system maps make dependencies and blind spots tangible.

Systemic Leadership: Consciously Shaping Roles, Patterns, and Relationships

Leadership in transformation requires special skills, such as recognizing patterns, consciously shaping roles, and tolerating blind spots in a system. Systemically minded managers can ask:

- What expectations are affecting me and my team—spoken or unspoken?
- Which relationship patterns in the team or organization keep the old ways stable?
- Which dynamics hinder change and which promote it?

In practice, this means doing less and enabling more. The chances of a successful transformation occurring increase when leaders create space for development instead of delegating change. Systemic leaders listen, observe closely, ask about context, and shape relationships in a way that allows new perspectives to emerge.

Resistance Is System Intelligence: How to Make Good Use of Disruptions

Resistance is often the system's most honest response to change. Not because people "don't want to," but because they have good reasons—from their perspective and based on their rational perceptions. Resistance indicates where the new idea has not been thought through, where trust is lacking, or where change is coming too quickly, too unclearly, or too contradictorily.

Seen through a system-oriented lens, resistance is therefore not a disruption—or even an obstacle— but a diagnostic tool. Feedback offers opportunities for further development of the organization. Those who take disruptions seriously learn more about the system and can make adjustments.

> **Example**
>
> The introduction of agile role models leads to unrest in a company. Managers view the emerging criticism as an obstacle. Only in a dialogue format does it become clear that many employees do not see agility as freedom but as uncertainty, because previous decision-making patterns remain unclear. In our example, resistance is therefore a result of the absence of a reference framework rather than due to a lack of motivation.

1.5 Thinking Ahead from the Outset: Corporate Culture as a Driver of Transformation

A successfully implemented transformation does not begin with new processes or technologies, but with people. They need an environment that actively promotes change. Transformation succeeds when it's built on a stable cultural foundation. Values, mindsets, and rituals determine whether innovations are accepted or rejected.

What Makes a Culture that Promotes Change?

- **It allows psychological security:** People need to feel that they can make mistakes without fear of negative consequences. Learning and experimentation are essential for change.
- **It enables change:** For example, in the form of innovation labs, experimentation rooms, and prototyping processes to try out new ways of working.
- **It focuses on transparency and communication:** Employees are actively involved in change, whether through open dialogue formats or "ask me anything" sessions with management.

- **It promotes the sharing of success stories:** People look to role models for guidance. Successful change-related projects should be shared to build trust and make change tangible.
- **It provides a framework for shared experiences and rituals:** Regular innovation "sprints," transformation days, or learning communities strengthen a shared understanding of change.

What to Do if the Corporate Culture Has Never Been Actively Shaped?
First of all, culture always exists, even when it has never been actively promoted, common values haven't been defined, or a vision hasn't been actively formulated. The culture that exists has grown organically, just like how people interact with one another, which has evolved over the course of a company's history.

So if all these areas have not been strategically considered up to now, the appropriate and necessary time to do so is at the latest before the next change process starts. The purpose, vision, mission, and values need to form the basis of the new direction.

Take active control of cultural development and provide your organization with impetus that will accompany the change process in an appropriate way.

Example

A company had no explicitly identifiable or even defined culture. After several acquisitions, a deficiency became apparent in this area. Employees were unsure of what to focus on. What would apply in the future? The values and rules of one company or the vision, mission, and leadership model of the second company? The company started with a survey and focus groups. This revealed that there was a particular desire for more personal responsibility and more open communication. The management responded with clear signals: it introduced regular feedback rounds and supported new ways of working. The first visible successes provided motivation and drove cultural development forward. Workshops focusing on a suitable shared vision, values that should apply to everyone, and guidelines for the new culture followed.

Cultural change requires clear steps:

1. **Assess the current situation:** Where do we stand? What do employees perceive as hindering or promoting progress?
2. **Develop a vision, mission, and values together:** Don't define these from the top down, but develop them through dialogue.
3. **Establish managers as cultural ambassadors:** They should lead by example.
4. **Use communication as a key tool:** Address change openly and keep it up for discussion.
5. **Achieve initial visible successes:** Small, noticeable changes build trust and momentum.

A high-performance culture is the decisive lever for an organization's success, especially in times of multiple crises and ongoing change and transformation. That's why we're devoting a separate chapter to this topic (Chap. 2).

1.6 Keeping the Target Group Firmly in View: Through a Systemic, Wide-Angle Lens

Let's stick with the example of a company introducing new software. The IT department is excited about the modern technology, but the customer service team worries that workflows will become more complicated. Without a systemic view, such resistance is often recognized too late.

A systemic approach helps to take target-group work to a new level. This is because every change is a complex interaction between people, structures, and processes. Different stakeholders have different expectations, fears, and needs. Target-group work entails not looking at communication in isolation, but at the system as a whole.

Personas Make Target Groups Tangible

In the transformation process, personas—illustrative representatives of the respective target groups—help to reduce complexity without simplifying it. They make tangible how different groups think, feel, and act, thereby enabling targeted communication, genuine participation, and effective measures. Instead of getting lost in generalities ("the employees," "the managers"), personas allow specific needs to be addressed:

- **"Anna, the customer expert"** (e.g., customer service team leader): Wants her customers to be satisfied and her employees to feel secure; needs clear instructions and room for questions.
- **"Markus, the tech enthusiast"** (e.g., IT process employee): Enthusiastic about new tools, but quickly loses interest when others don't follow suit.
- **"Fatima, the bridge-builder"** (e.g., communications officer): Wants to mediate between management and staff, but needs reliable information and access to managers to do so.
- **"Lena, the confidante"** (e.g., production team leader): Often seen as an informal point of contact, can influence change positively or negatively, depending on how effectively she's involved.
- **"Stefan, the pragmatist" (e.g., accounting clerk):** Is rather critical of innovations and often questions their necessity; needs clear economic arguments and measurable results to be convinced.

Personas make communication with the target groups behind them more targeted and therefore more effective. Formats hit the mark better, and managers can be empowered in a targeted way because expectations of them during change are clearly stated and supported. In short, personas turn target groups into genuine dialogue partners. They promote systemic thinking on a small scale and enable effective change on a large scale.

From Analysis to Implementation: Effectively Involving Target Groups
A systemic view and clearly defined personas are the starting point—but it's only the right involvement that makes the difference. After all, good target-group work doesn't just stop at analysis. It addresses the question: How do I shape change *with* people—not without them?

There are three principles of effective work relating to stakeholders:

1. Networked systemic thinking:
   Every change has side effects—a new technology, for example, can simplify processes but at the same time trigger job fears. Those who recognize dependencies and interactions at an early stage can make smarter decisions.
2. Participation as a factor for success:
   People are more likely to accept change if they're allowed to help shape it. Participation reduces resistance and increases identification with change.
3. Take dynamics into account:
   Companies are constantly changing—and so are their stakeholders. One-off stakeholder management is not enough; it needs to be reviewed continuously (at least every 6 months) and, ideally, adapted.

How to Successfully Integrate Stakeholders in Practice

1. **Understand needs—before resistance arises:**
   Transformation aims to make a company more future-proof. If employees are to accept this, organizations need to get a feel for the fears and expectations of all those involved at an early stage. The following can help:

   - Surveys and interviews to identify needs.
   - Personas that are also discussed with the target groups.
   - Design thinking workshops to develop creative solutions.
   - Stakeholder mapping to understand interactions.

2. **Develop a smart engagement and communication strategy:**
   Early involvement builds trust and reduces resistance. A good communication strategy (see also Chap. 4 answers three questions:

   - **Who?** Which groups are affected or have influence?
   - **When?** In which phases is their involvement crucial?
   - **How?** What types of involvement are appropriate for which groups?

3. **Set measurable milestones:**
   Without clear indicators, change remains a gut feeling. Companies should define KPIs to measure progress and impact:

   - **Employee satisfaction:** Is trust in the transformation increasing?
   - **Willingness to change:** How broad is the acceptance of new processes?
   - **Degree of innovation:** Are new ideas being introduced and implemented?

Regular evaluations enable adjustments and ensure sustainable results.

1.7   Well Planned Is half the Battle: The Change Roadmap

Change is a highly structured process. Ideally. One of the most frequently cited approaches comes from **John P. Kotter** (Kotter, 1996), who created a standard with his 8-step model (see Sect. 1.3). A 30/90/360-day road-map based on his approach helps put a timeframe on the (first) months of change in transformation projects in a smart way.

At the beginning of the planning process, you conducted surveys, identified communication needs, defined target groups, and developed personas. All of these findings must then be brought together in the change roadmap. Who needs what information, why, and by when? And how often should updates be provided?

Here's a brief look at the general phases of a classic transformation process:

1. **The first 30 days** are all about providing orientation, highlighting urgency, and building trust. The need for change should be communicated clearly and emotionally—with data, analysis, and strong narratives. Target visions are developed, stakeholders are involved, and managers are prepared for their role as change agents.

2. **Between days 31 and 90**, the activation phase follows: initial visible measures and quick wins create credibility, obstacles are removed, and employees are actively involved. Exchange formats such as "change cafés" and internal success stories support this process.
3. **From day 90 onwards**, the focus is on consolidation: new processes are firmly established, progress is measured, culture is developed in a targeted manner, and managers receive long-term support. The new becomes the norm—made visible through stories of success and lessons learned, effective and deeply rooted in day-to-day working lives.

1.8   Plan Pit Stops: Leading and Changing Also Means Taking a Look at Yourself

Change doesn't just affect the workforce. It also affects those who are supposed to provide guidance: management, executives, organizational developers, communicators, and HR experts. Times of change reveal how crucial the ability to lead oneself is. After all, if you want to lead through change, you first have to be able to lead yourself. This means:

* Being aware of where you stand in terms of mindset, skills, and resistance.
* Knowing your own drivers.
* Sensing what makes us feel insecure.

Only then can we remain capable of acting, even when the outside world is in turmoil. This isn't a luxury, it's a necessary everyday strategy. Teams can sense whether leadership is clear, stable, and authentic—or not. Self-leadership creates precisely this inner stability and thus the necessary credibility toward the outside world. Because:

* Those who understand themselves are better able to respond to others.
* Those who regulate themselves encounter resistance with greater confidence.
* Those who can motivate themselves remain powerful even when situations become complex or uncomfortable.

This is exactly where coaching and sparring sessions come in. They offer space for reflection, for self-assessment, and for consciously developing your own attitude. Not as a weakness, but as a strength—and as an active contribution to a culture of change.

What Works Well?

- When coaching starts at the very top: a board of directors that talks openly about its reflections appears stronger, not weaker.
- When coaching is seen not as a deficit but as a performance booster: "Clarity in leadership and communication is my job."
- When there are low-threshold formats: peer coaching, sparring, shadowing, walk & talks.
- When communication and HR staff take joint responsibility—and don't leave leadership to its own devices.

A Suggestion from Practice
Would you like to give your organization a positive boost right at the start of a change process? Then let moderators and coaches accompany you as management and discuss it internally. It's not about technology or transformation tools but about attitude, clarity, and self-management. The effect? Noticeable. In communication, in decisions, in cooperation. And thus, in the credibility of change.

1.9 Takeaways

Transformation isn't achieved through appropriate measures alone; it begins with people. It requires a vision that provides orientation, communication that inspires, and a culture that not only allows change but enables it. Leadership is not just about external control, but above all about self-management from within. Those who want to shape change must understand the needs of stakeholders, be able to tolerate contradictions, and lead with conviction. Because change isn't just a project—it's a shared journey.

- **Transformation is much more than change**: It affects the structures, identity, attitude, and culture of a company.
- **Communication creates connection**: As well as information, people need real-life mission statements, appropriate stories, and genuine dialogue to get on board.
- **Culture is a decisive factor for success in change processes**: Transformation needs spaces where new approaches can be tried out, mistakes can be made, and lessons can be learned together.

References

Beckhard, R., & Harris, R. T. (1977). *Organizational transitions: Managing complex change*. Addison-Wesley.

Kotter, J. P. (1996). *Leading change*. Harvard Business School Press.

Streich, R. (2016). *Change management: Fundamentals and success factors*. Springer Gabler.

2

Culture as a Force Field: Why Culture Determines whether Transformation Succeeds

Three key points:

1. **Culture is never neutral:**
   It's there and it has an effect—whether we actively shape it or not. Culture can accelerate or block change. Those who ignore it lose out—at the latest when change fails to "take hold."
2. **Behavior is culture in action:**
   Culture manifests itself in everyday life. In decisions, meetings, conflicts, e-mail exchanges, and break-time conversations—in how we interact with each other.
3. **Cultural change is not a sprint:**
   If you want to change culture, you need patience, dialogue, and role models. And you need to understand that every cultural development also involves micropolitics, uncertainty, and emotional energy.

Culture is the invisible operating system of every organization. It determines how people feel and act—often without them even realizing it. Decisions, communication, conflicting behavior, courage to innovate, or dealing with mistakes: all of these are expressions of the culture that's being lived.

Especially in change projects, culture isn't just a "soft" add-on—it's the decisive lever. It influences:

- How open people are to new ideas and how they use feedback for further development.
- Whether employees think for themselves or play it safe.
- Whether leadership promotes or hinders change.

> **Example**
>
> A company wants to become more agile. It creates flat hierarchies and cross-functional teams. But silence continues to dominate meetings, decisions are "pushed upward" and real responsibility is avoided. The reason: a culture of caution that has developed over many years—and managers who advocate "empowerment" but then make decisions themselves whenever there is uncertainty. The result: the agile operating system does not work—because the cultural operating system is not compatible.

2.1 Values, Attitudes, Behavior: How Culture Emerges and Works

Culture develops wherever people come together. It can't be "decided"—it evolves through habits, informal rules, and collective experiences.

American social scientist Edgar Schein describes three levels of this:

1. **Artifacts**: Everything visible—dress codes, architecture, language, internal communication formats. These show how an organization wants to be seen.
2. **Values**: What's consciously considered desirable—for example, customer focus and personal responsibility. These values are often set out in mission statements.
3. **Basic assumptions**: The unconscious. Deeply held beliefs—such as "you can't make mistakes here" or "only those who conform get ahead." These shape the actual culture.

If companies want cultural change, they must address all three levels. A new mission statement (values) is not enough if behavior (artifacts) and basic assumptions do not follow suit.

The Graves model helps to classify developments culturally: from authoritarian-hierarchical to performance-oriented to value-driven or co-creative. It makes it clear that every organization has its own level of maturity—and every transformation must take this level of maturity into account.

2.2 The Graves Levels: Understanding the Cultural DNA of Organizations

The Graves model, which became known through "Spiral Dynamics" (Beck & Cowan, 1996), among other works, describes how value systems develop in individuals, teams, and entire organizations. It assumes that people respond to novel challenges with new ways of thinking—and that these ways of thinking repeat themselves in certain patterns. They can be described as **color codes**, each of which embodies a particular world view, set of values, and way of organizing.

The model is **not a step-by-step plan** to be "worked through." Rather, these attitudes often coexist side by side—and it's worthwhile to find out **which ones dominate**, **where conflicts arise as a result**, and **what's needed culturally** to really drive transformation forward.

The Graves Levels and Their Organizational Logic
Purple—magic, belonging
(hardly dominant in modern organizations, but noticeable, for example, in the sense of "clan thinking" or "family feeling")

- **World view:** "The group protects me—and I obey it."
- **Characteristics:** Strong identification with tradition, community, where belonging is more important than performance.
- **Examples:** Traditional family businesses, including start-ups in the early stages of founding.

Red—power and strength

- **Guiding principle:** Assertiveness.
- **World view:** "I take what I need."
- **Typical of:** Milieus or organizations with a strongly dominant culture. Decisions are based on power logic, not structure.
- **Visible in organizations through:** Authoritarian leadership, zero tolerance for mistakes, loyalty above all else.
- **Examples:** Military units on deployment, first-generation family businesses with a patriarchal structure.

In transformation processes, red is often a "disturbance signal": resistance to participation or reduction in hierarchy.

Blue—order and rules

- **Guiding principle:** Security through structure.
- **World view:** "There's one right way to do things."
- **Typical for:** Administrations, authorities, government-related companies. Decisions follow rules and processes.
- **Characteristics:** Clear hierarchies, responsibilities, "committee logic."
- **Examples:** Companies with official structures.

Blue creates stability—but can quickly appear too rigid in dynamic markets. Change is only accepted if it's formally legitimized.

Orange—performance and success

- **Guiding principle:** Success and growth through competition.
- **World view:** "Those who achieve more get ahead."
- **Typical for:** Sales organizations, consulting firms, ambitious corporations.
- **Characteristics:** Goal orientation, KPI-oriented logic, efficiency, innovation.
- **Examples:** Management consultancies, start-ups with scalable business models, large sales units.

Orange drives innovation—but can be socially exhausting. Without orange (and blue), however, companies struggle to achieve efficiency and financial success.

Green—community and values

- **Guiding principle:** Equality and participation.
- **World view:** "True strength comes from working together."
- **Typical for:** NGOs, value-oriented companies, agile organizations.
- **Characteristics:** Flat hierarchies, culture of consensus, psychological safety.
- **Examples:** Socially oriented companies, companies with sociocracy or holacracy, some cooperatives.

Green promotes trust—but can lead to indecisiveness. In "green cultures," seemingly endless rounds of consultation threaten to replace clear direction.

Yellow—systemic thinking and personal responsibility

- **Guiding principle:** Meaning and development.
- **World view:** "Complexity requires context awareness."
- **Typical for:** Learning organizations, companies with a strong culture of reflection and decentralized control.
- **Characteristics:** Integrative leadership, learning orientation, high degree of self-control.
- **Examples:** Selected transformation projects in large corporations, innovation areas in tech companies.

Yellow manages to penetrate high levels of complexity. Trust, maturity, and personal responsibility characterize these cultures.

Turquoise and coral—wholeness and planetary responsibility

Still quite rare, more commonly used as a strategic compass

- **Mindset:** Cross-system, evolutionary, purpose-driven, wanting to make a difference.

Turquoise structures are rare and may be difficult for some to understand.

What Does this Mean for your Organization?
Every organization "ticks" differently—and brings its own mix of colors to the table, for example:

- **Sales units** often live strongly in orange (goals, numbers, competition).
- **Consulting firms** often combine orange (performance), green (cooperation), and yellow (lifelong learning).
- **Government agencies** are usually strongly blue (rules, structure), with individual green islands (participation).
- **Start-ups** often start out green (meaning, relationships)—and then have to learn blue and orange more frequently (focus, clarity of goals).

During transformation, it's important to look at your own situation in both the long and short term: What colors dominate in which areas, and which values are therefore lived out? How compatible are we? Where are "development leaps" emerging that are overwhelming us and our employees?

A green company that suddenly wants to lead in a yellow way ("self-organization") will fail if it lacks fundamental clarity of purpose (orange). A classic blue company that introduces agile methods first needs spaces where psychological safety (green) can develop in the first place.

Please keep this in mind: There's no "better" or "worse," no "further along than others." A field located lower in the chart is not worse than the one above it. In a successful company, employees feel they belong (purple), are performance-oriented (orange), and follow the idea of lifelong learning (yellow). It's important to regularly check which levels are currently prominent in everyday life and how the characteristics of the individual fields fit in with the respective strategy (Fig. 2.1).

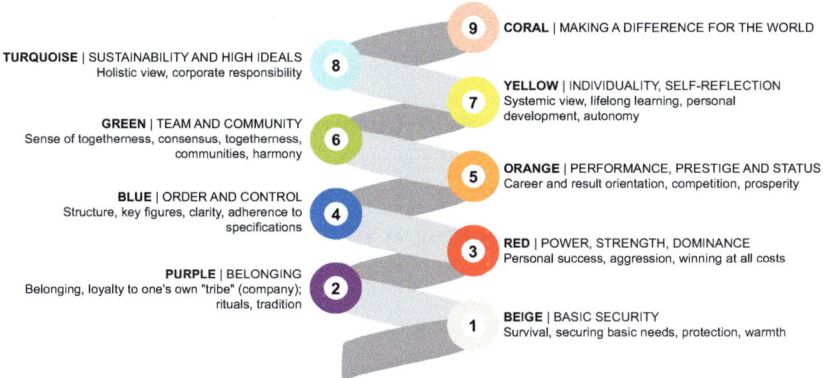

Fig. 2.1 The Graves levels according to Clare Graves: "Graves Model" and 9-level system by Rainer Krumm (authors' own representation)

2.3   How One Thing Leads to Another: Leadership, Communication, and Collaboration Together Shape Culture

Culture emerges from daily interactions: How do people work together? How do they communicate? How are decisions made? How are people led? Who's allowed to be loud—and who isn't?

Specific Cultural Drivers in Everyday Life

- In leadership: Distribution of power, decision-making patterns, error culture.
- In communication: Openness, choice of channels, flow of information.
- In collaboration: Dealing with conflicts, role clarification, trust.

Example

There's a culture of "don't stand out" in a company. Innovation is lacking. Interviews reveal that employees hold back because previous ideas were publicly criticized and there are no appreciative correction procedures. The culture of communications and leadership prevents new ideas from emerging, even though they're described as "desirable" in the strategy document.

Ask yourself: What cultural messages does your organization send out—consciously and unconsciously?

Culture Diagnosis: How to Make Culture Visible

Culture is often tangible but difficult to grasp—that's why tools are needed to help identify typical patterns, blind spots, and contradictions.

Three effective ways of looking at your own culture:

- **Qualitative**

  - In-depth interviews with employees at all levels.
  - Shadowing: Silent observation of meetings, processes, and informal interactions.
  - Culture workshops using narrative methods: "When was the last time you felt proud of working here?"

- **Quantitative**

  - Standardized culture assessments (e.g., Denison, Barrett).
  - Pulse surveys with culture indicators (e.g., psychological safety, trust, openness).

- **Systemic**

  - Stakeholder mapping to reveal micropolitics.
  - Symbol analysis: What's "rewarded" and what's "punished"?
  - Resonance chambers: What's said—and what isn't?

Tip for implementation:

Start with qualitative methods—they build trust, provide depth, and open up dialogue. Quantitative data can be used in parallel or later to validate trends and measure changes.

2.4   Trust and Team Health

Where trust is lacking, conflicts remain unresolved, learning curves remain flat, and communication is superficial and noncommittal, this can have major impacts on individuals, teams, and companies. If a team remains in this state for a long time, it won't just be ineffective—it will become unhealthy. Two models help us visualize the state of a team and work on it in a targeted manner: the dysfunction model and the trust tree.

What Blocks Trust: The Five Dysfunctions of a Team
Patrick Lencioni has developed one of the most influential models for teamwork—now a classic in the context of leadership. He describes five levels at which teams can fail.

The dysfunctions build upon one another like a pyramid—and each level has consequences for the next:

1. **Lack of trust:**
   The root of all evil. If team members don't have the courage to admit weaknesses or show uncertainty, a culture of caution develops. Openness becomes the exception rather than the norm.
2. **Fear of conflict:**
   Those who lack trust avoid friction. Discussions are superficial, and differences of opinion are sat out rather than resolved. And this happens precisely where genuine debate would be productive.
3. **Lack of commitment:**
   Where there is no open discussion, there is no real commitment. Decisions are accepted rather than supported. People go along with things—half-heartedly.
4. **Avoidance of responsibility:**
   Those who have not been involved in the decision-making process don't feel responsible. Responsibility is shifted onto others—for results as well as for your own behavior.
5. **Inattention to results:**
   When no one's concerned about the common goal any more, individual interests become the benchmark. Personal success counts for more than the team result. And at some point, everyone notices this.

Reflection Prompt
This model is ideal for teams off-site or for leadership workshops. Work with your team along the five levels: Where are we? Where are the sticking points? Where are dynamics emerging that are blocking us? And be sure to start at the bottom—with trust. Everything else builds on that.

How Trust Grows: The Trust Tree
While Lencioni shows what can happen when trust is lacking and dysfunctional structures arise, Stephen M. R. Covey provides the counterpart: a well-founded answer to the question *"How does trust actually develop?"* and what can I, as a manager, do to promote it?

His model takes trust as a strategic factor for success. It doesn't grow by chance but instead follows principles. These principles can be represented as a "trust tree" with roots, trunk, branches, and fruit.

- **Integrity (the roots):**
  Without integrity, there can be no lasting trust. Those who don't "walk the talk" lose credibility. Honesty, value orientation, and attitude are the cornerstones of the foundation.
- **Intent (the trunk):**
  People trust when they feel that someone means well by them. This has to do with transparency, a focus on the common good, and comprehensible motives. Those who clearly show why they're doing something—and for whom—appear trustworthy.
- **Ability (the branches):**
  Trust requires competence. If I feel that the person I'm dealing with is capable, then I trust them more. Experience, knowledge, and a willingness to learn make the tree stable.
- **Results (the fruit):**
  Trust becomes visible when announcements turn into actions and actions turn into results. Those who deliver on what they promise strengthen trust in the organization—a little bit more every day.

Reflection Prompt
Use the trust tree as a mirror for your management team. Ask yourself:

- How honest are we really?
- Are our intentions clearly recognizable—for employees, customers, stakeholders?
- Do we have the necessary expertise in the team—and do we demonstrate it?
- And lastly: Do we deliver what we promise?

2.5 Psychological Safety: The Invisible Foundation for Change

Change always means dealing with fears and a sense of "risk." Opinions, ideas, your own position: all of these can be subject to change and are thus "at stake." The issue of whether people reveal themselves, get involved, or prefer to remain silent during these uncertain phases is a decisive factor in the success or failure of a change project.

Psychological safety is therefore the central concept and desire for every organization. Organizational researcher **Amy Edmondson** has helped shape this concept, defining psychological safety as:

A shared belief that the team is safe for interpersonal risk-taking. (Amy C. Edmondson, The Fearless Organization, 2019).

This refers to a shared understanding within a team that it's okay to show who you are—without fear of being devalued, embarrassed, or suffering negative consequences. It represents the safe environment that enables people to ask questions, admit mistakes, express ideas—and disagree.

Without this security, the organization remains in a pattern of self-censorship: smart thoughts are not shared, critical comments go unvoiced, and experiences are not reflected upon. The result: innovative strength, learning ability, and energy for change fall by the wayside.

How Psychological Safety Can be Strengthened in a Targeted Way

Psychological safety doesn't arise "just like that." It's the result of conscious leadership, clear communication, and a respectful approach to mistakes. Here are five specific measures for managers and change managers:

1. Actively practice tolerance for mistakes:

   "What's allowed here?"—employees often ask themselves this question without saying it out loud. Managers who talk openly about their own mistakes encourage others to do the same.

2. Signal curiosity – don't just "radiate" knowledge:

   Managers don't have to know everything. But they do have to show that they want to learn. Questions such as *"What are we overlooking?"* or *"How do you see it?"* open up space for participation.

3. Appreciate dissent:

   When employees are courageous and think "against the grain," it's a gift—not a risk. Leadership that handles criticism confidently strengthens trust.

4. Make psychological safety a rule in meetings

   Establish meeting standards in which all perspectives are explicitly welcome—for instance, through check-ins, a "last word" round, or an explicit invitation to express opposing views.

5. Consciously send micro-signals

   How you respond to contributions shapes the culture. Nodding, interrupting, showing appreciation, remaining silent—these are all "cultural signals." Pay attention to what you say. And what you don't say.

Reflection Prompt for Change Managers and Leadership Teams

- Where do we observe self-censorship?
- In what situations is constructive criticism expressed—and where is it not?
- How do managers respond to mistakes and uncertainty?
- What would have to happen for more people in this organization to feel comfortable expressing their opinions?

2.6 Changing Culture: Why there Are no Shortcuts

Cultural change doesn't mean just communicating an agreeable new vision: "Look, this is our new culture." Shaping culture means developing a new normal, presenting it, making it tangible, and then, step by step, anchoring it in everyday life.

What Cultural Work Needs

- **Patience:** Culture changes through behavior, not through announcements.
- **Role models:** Leaders send the strongest signals in a system.
- **Continuity:** Cultural change requires rituals, repetition, and reinforcement.

Practical Tips for your Planning

- Start with the diagnosis—not with the target vision (so as not to over-whelm the organization in the end).
- Define cultural guidelines together with key individuals.
- Use every measure (meetings, e-mails, feedback) as a cultural signal.
- Communicate "small victories"—these strengthen credibility.
- Expect setbacks—they're part of the process.

Important: Cultural contradictions ("We want more responsibility, but all decisions are still made by department heads") should be addressed—not glossed over. Otherwise, trust will be lost.

2.7   Takeaways

- Culture is the invisible but most powerful lever for or against change.
- It shows itself in everyday life—not in mission statements.
- If you want to change culture, you first have to understand it—and then patiently guide it.
- Leadership, communication, and cooperation are the day-to-day tools for cultural change.
- Cultural change begins with us—in every e-mail, every decision, every reaction.

References

Beck, D. E., & Cowan, C. C. (1996). Spiral dynamics: Mastering values. *Leadership, and Change.*

Covey, Stephen M. R. (2006). *The Speed of Trust, Free Press.* Graphic idea: https://trustedge.com/stephen-mr-covey-trust-tree/

Edgar H. Schein & Peter Schein. (2021). *Organizational Culture and Leadership.* Vahlen Verlag, 6th edition.

Edmondson, Amy C. (2019). *The fearless organization: How to create psychological safety at work for greater development, learning, and innovation (Vahlen Verlag, 2020).* Original: The Fearless Organization.

Lencioni, Patrick (2002). *The Five Dysfunctions of a Team.* Jossey-Bass.

3

Motivation and Needs of Employees in Change Processes

Three key points:

1. **Individual approach as a catalyst for change:**
   People are motivated by different things and want to be addressed individually.
2. **Emotional security creates trust:**
   Resistance to change processes arises from, among other problems, a lack of trust. Providing psychological security creates a foundation and scope for development.
3. **Ownership beats instruction:**
   Change succeeds when employees say, "This is my change, too." Participation and relevance are the keys to genuine responsibility.

Change can inspire—or deter. It can be viewed either as an opportunity or as a threat. How employees react depends not only on the nature of the change but mainly on how it's communicated, accompanied, and made tangible. Motivation is the decisive factor here: those who feel seen and valued are more likely to embrace change. But what motivates people exactly? What needs do employees have? And what levers can be used to

A. Montua, *Guiding Transformation*, Business Guides on the Go, https://doi.org/10.1007/978-3-658-49755-2_3

actively involve employees in the change process and strengthen their trust in management and their commitment?

Example

Daniel K. has been head of internal communications at a large retail company for 5 years. Business has been stable so far, but now radical change is on the horizon: bricks-and-mortar retail is losing market share while online sales are growing rapidly. Management has decided to make the company more digital—with new e-commerce platforms, automation in logistics, and increased use of AI for personalized customer communication. But as the strategy takes shape, resistance is growing among the teams. The biggest challenges:

- **Uncertainty among the workforce**: Many employees are wondering whether their jobs will still be needed in the future. Anxiety is particularly prevalent in stores and in traditional sales.
- **"We've always done it this way" mentality**: The corporate culture is shaped by long-standing employees who are proud of tried-and-tested processes. Change is seen as a threat, not an opportunity.
- **Lack of identification with change**: Communication about the transformation has been top-down so far. Employees feel left out and presented with a fait accompli.
- **Skepticism toward digital solutions**: Many teams lack the expertise for new technologies. There's a widespread fear of no longer being able to find one's way in our digital world.

Daniel K. realizes that a few PowerPoint charts and e-mails won't be enough to successfully accompany this change. He needs a communication strategy that takes into account the phases of change and the emotions of employees, builds trust, addresses fears, and enables participation. But how can he achieve this?

3.1 Understanding Needs: Why Change Often Generates Resistance

Our minds love routines. Because they make us feel good—and because they save energy. Change, on the other hand, means adapting to new situations, abandoning familiar patterns, and enduring uncertainty. No wonder many of us initially react with skepticism or rejection when a new process of change or transformation is announced.

But resistance isn't always resistance. It's often a sign of unmet, unseen, or unheard needs. There are six core needs that are often touched upon in change processes:

1. **Desire for joy:** People want to feel joy, pleasure, and "flow" in what they do. In change processes, however, the issues that make us feel frustrated about our daily tasks often predominate.
2. **Desire for security:** People want security in their everyday lives. What's there today should still be there tomorrow, if possible. Change, on the other hand, creates uncertainty: What do these new developments mean for me? Will I keep my job? Will my responsibilities change? Will I get new colleagues?
3. **Desire for autonomy:** People want to act autonomously. Changes viewed as "dictated from above" are therefore often met with resentment.
4. **Desire for belonging:** We want to feel that we belong—to a group, a team, an organization. In situations of change, much is new.
5. **Desire for fairness:** If a change is seen as unfair (for example, a perceived unequal distribution of opportunities), resistance increases.
6. **Desire for self-fulfillment:** We want to feel that what we do has meaning and want to be able to help shape issues. In situations of change, this need is often disappointed, especially when there is little room for participation and input.

Those who are aware of basic human needs and take them into account in (change) communication can often defuse much resistance in advance. A change of perspective often helps: How would I react to such a change myself? What uncertainties would I have? What information would I need to feel secure?

It's also worth taking a look at an organization's "legacy issues": Have many changes been implemented in the past that were not communicated appropriately? Did this perhaps leave a bad taste in people's mouths, and could the current resistance to change or even "change fatigue" be rooted in these unresolved issues? Employees may then no longer believe that a new change could really be meaningful or sustainable. There's only one action that can truly help here: consistently working through these legacy issues and learning from the mistakes of the past.

3.2   Increasing the Momentum for Change: Knowing the Levers of Motivation

In order to respond optimally to people's needs in change processes, it's helpful to know their motives. In our accompanying coaching and leadership work, we use the so-called Luxx/Reiss profiles to look at this topic in an individualized way.

Steven Reiss, an American psychologist, conducted intensive research into human motivation until his death a few years ago. This research resulted in a scheme comprising 16 life motives. Knowing these motives and taking them into account in change processes can make communication and leadership much more effective (Fig. 3.1).

We'd now like to present five of the most relevant motives for transformation in a professional context. A more in-depth overview of all motives is summarized in our book *"Führungsaufgabe Interne Kommunikation"* (*Leadership Task: Internal Communications*).

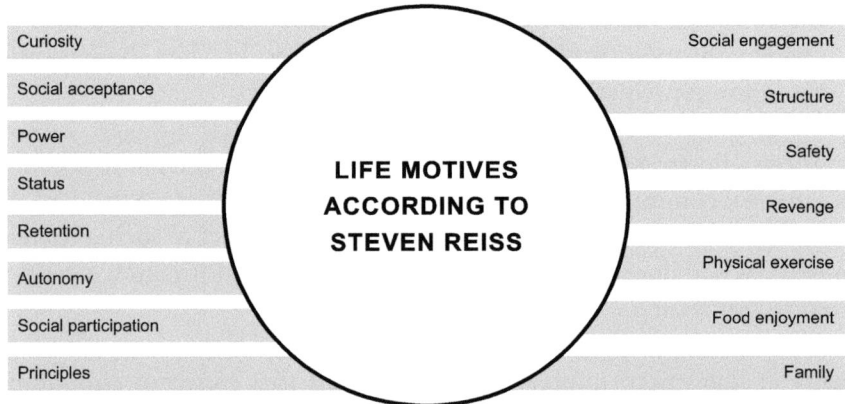

Fig. 3.1 Life motives according to Steven Reiss (source: author's own representation)

- **Motivation—influence/power**: Shows how strong someone's desire is to actively shape situations, make decisions, and have a noticeable impact.
- **Independence (autonomy) motive**: Describes the need to be able to act in an emotionally free manner, independently, and autonomously from others.
- **Social contact motive**: Provides information about how important to us are new connections/relationships, friendships, and social interaction beyond work.
- **Motivation structure**: Describes the individual desire for order, planning, and reliability.
- **Security motive**: Shows how important peace, stability, and predictability are to us—or whether we find new situations and changes more stimulating.

In order to win people over to change, change-related measures should also be specifically targeted. Let's look at three examples:

1. **Transparency:** People need clear explanations. Why is this change necessary? What will happen if we don't change anything? And what does this mean for each individual? Open, honest communication builds trust and reduces uncertainty.
2. **Co-creation/participation:** Employees want to have a say. If they're involved at an early stage and can contribute to the change themselves, acceptance increases. Participation is key to willingness to change.
3. **Success stories:** Change becomes tangible when initial progress, known as "quick wins," becomes visible. Small, measurable successes help to build motivation and reduce fear of the new.

3.3 How Fears Can be Made Visible and Addressed

Resistance to change is usually not a sign of stubbornness or unwillingness but has deeper causes, such as fears and uncertainties. These often remain unspoken. Employees may fear, for example:

- **Job loss or loss of status**: "Will I still be relevant after the change?"
- **Being overwhelmed**: "Can I meet the new requirements?"
- **Lack of control**: "I don't know what to expect."
- **Skepticism about leadership or strategy**: "Do they really have a plan?"

The problem is that many employees don't express these concerns openly—whether out of fear of negative consequences, because they themselves don't yet know exactly what's worrying them, or because there appears to be no room for such concerns to be aired in the prevailing corporate culture.

Managers can and should make these fears visible. Waiting for employees to come forward on their own will usually be unsuccessful. Instead, targeted tools can be used to gauge the mood within the team and to address anxieties proactively.

Methods for Identifying and Addressing Fears

- **Anonymous mood barometers**: Digital feedback tools or brief "pulse checks" let managers derive an initial picture of the mood without individuals having to expose themselves.
- **Open dialogue sessions**: Employees can express their concerns in moderated discussions. It's crucial to create an atmosphere of trust here.
- **Individual conversations**: Some fears are very personal—in these cases, it helps to listen in a one-on-one setting and offer targeted support.
- **Storytelling**: Success stories from colleagues who have already faced and overcome similar changes can alleviate fears and encourage others.

Resistance is often a cry for help. Managers who understand that fear is behind it can address it specifically and support employees throughout the various phases of change.

3.4   Personnel Development: Empowering People and Providing Guidance

Change can only succeed if employees are able to find their paths in the new reality. This means that they need not only to be informed but also empowered. Training, coaching, and targeted development measures help employees to see new developments as opportunities rather than threats.

But empowerment goes beyond mere technical training. It's also about providing emotional security. Managers should offer guidance and be available as sparring partners. Open Q&A sessions, peer coaching, or mentoring help to accompany employees on their pathways through change.

Targeted skills development is also worthwhile: What new skills does the team need for the future? Which soft skills are crucial? Continuing education and training programs can be tailored to address these issues.

3.5   How Employees Can View Change Processes as "their" Change

The difference between "I have to go along with this change" and "I'm part of this change" is the key to successful transformation. Because when people experience change as a process in which they can play a role, they don't feel driven, but rather like creators—and that's precisely what increases motivation and commitment. When employees feel that they have influence over the process, they're more likely to take responsibility and actively work to make the change a success.

Three factors governing success:

1. **Involvement from the outset:**
    Many change processes fail because employees are only informed once everything has already been decided. However, those who are involved at an early stage—through early explanations of "why we're changing," workshops, dialogue formats, or co-creation processes—

not only feel heard but also part of the change. This strengthens identification and commitment.

2. **Enable personal responsibility:**

Ownership requires room for maneuver. Employees should not only be allowed to give feedback, but also have genuine opportunities to help shape the process. Workshops in which they devise and test solutions themselves can be useful for this purpose. The more influence someone has on the change, the more responsible they feel for its success.

3. **Establish personal relevance:**

People only commit to change if they understand what it will bring them. Managers should therefore explain to each person: How will I personally benefit from this transformation? What opportunities will it create for me? Direct conversations are helpful here, as is storytelling—for example, colleagues reporting on how they've used the change as an opportunity.

3.6   Takeaways

Change can only succeed if it's designed *with* people, not against them. Information, motivation, and empowerment are the keys to breaking down resistance and shaping change successfully. Those who focus on transparency, participation, and a sense of achievement, who take worries seriously and involve employees at an early stage, can establish change as a joint process.

- Resistance is often a sign of unmet basic needs, such as security, autonomy, or belonging.
- Psychological safety is not a soft factor, but the hard currency for successful transformation.
- Turning employees into co-creators instead of those affected brings about the decisive shift—from "I have to…" to "I'm happy to be part of it."

4

The Roles of Leadership, Communications, and HR

Three key points:

1. **Leadership and communications determine the success of change**:
    Strategies and structures are important. However, change can only reveal its full potential with the support of managers.
2. **Employees need clarity and involvement**:
    This is because change creates uncertainty. If you want to shape change successfully, you have to explain it clearly, involve employees, and enable them to play a genuine role in shaping it whenever possible.
3. **Resistance is normal – and an opportunity:**
    People often react skeptically to change. Leadership can take these fears seriously, build trust, and demonstrate tangible benefits.

In change processes especially, managers need not only to develop strategies but also bring people on board. But how does this work in practice? What challenges arise when employees are uncertain or resistant to change? And how does a manager navigate the balancing act between corporate goals and team dynamics?

A. Montua, *Guiding Transformation*, Business Guides on the Go, https://doi.org/10.1007/978-3-658-49755-2_4

Example

Martin K. has been a team leader in a medium-sized technology company for 15 years. He knows the industry inside out, and his team values him for his reliability and expertise. But times are changing: the company needs to become more agile, develop new digital business models, and keep pace with an increasingly fast-moving market. The management decides on a comprehensive transformation—away from rigid hierarchies and toward more personal responsibility and interdisciplinary teams.

Martin's biggest challenge is that his team feels unsettled. Many employees fear that they won't be able to keep up with the new requirements or that their jobs will disappear. He himself feels torn between the expectations of management and the concerns of his employees.

The first change-related measures are met with resistance. Some employees refuse to adopt the new ways of working, while others retreat into silence. Martin realizes that information meetings alone aren't enough—personal contact, understanding, and opportunities for discussion are needed.

4.1   Role Models and Points of Contact: The Role of Managers

Good leadership in change processes is not demonstrated in grandiose speeches but in everyday life, in moments when employees feel uncertain. In conversations where questions remain unanswered. In the willingness to listen, explain, and deal with uncomfortable issues, and even to reflect on your own actions.

What Tasks Should Managers Take on in Change Processes?

- **Build trust**: Not only in the vision for change, but also in themselves as leaders. And in their ability to accompany change.
- **Translate strategies**: Generalized statements such as "We need to become more agile" or "Digitalization is our future" remain empty if they remain intangible. Managers have to explain what this means specifically for everyday work.

- **Take emotions seriously**: Fear, doubt, resistance—these are not disruptions but signals. If you want to lead, you have to be able to work with emotions—not against them.
- **Be present**: Not just in meetings, but wherever uncertainty arises. Even in passing.
- **Use storytelling**: Stories stick, facts often don't. The "why" must be explained before the "what" follows.

Example

When a new tool is introduced, many people first think of the extra work it will involve. However, much more important than the function itself (what does it do) is how the tool reduces workload, minimizes errors, or saves time (why did we purchase it). This way, it doesn't become another problem, but part of the "solution."

4.2   Driving Change Together: The Role of Communications and HR

Leadership is important—but it needs support from internal communications and other colleagues in communications to provide tools and formats, take care of communicating processes and results, and enable (virtual) space for dialogue. HR also translates the change-related strategy into contracts and processes, plans journeys for employees, and takes care of roles and skill sets. No area can or should act without the other—and certainly not against each other.

The joint operational spectrum is broad:

- **Developing a vision and narrative:** The change strategy must be placed in its overall context and translated into communicable messages.
- **Identifying needs and potential:** Which areas, managers, and employees have what needs and requirements in the change process, and how can these be addressed through communication?
- **Supporting leadership:** Not every manager is a natural communicator. Internal communications provides the toolbox: PowerPoint templates, argumentation aids, guidelines, storylines, and much more.

- **Creating clarity**: Contradictory messages lead to uncertainty. Planned and accompanying communication ensures consistency—in language, timing, and tone.
- **Think about target groups**: Not every team member needs the same information. Communication translates messages for the various stakeholders—from the board level to colleagues in the factories.
- **Enable dialogue**: Change requires exchange. Communication creates formats, platforms, and opportunities for this.
- **Address emotions**: Facts inform, stories move. Narratives ensure that the change process is emotionally anchored.
- **Recognize moods**: Those who listen understand more. Communication is also an early warning system—for flagging up uncertainty, frustration, or silent resistance.
- **Help shape culture**: Communication helps shape the image of change. Culture translates change in formats, tools, and messages—not just in strategy papers, but in everyday life.

4.3   A Tool to Pass on: The 5-Minute Leadership Task

Managers in change processes need more time. While the need for communication within teams increases massively, managers' own time shrinks due to their increased workloads.

Many of them are therefore looking for efficient ways to establish empathetic communication as a fixed ritual in their everyday work. This is where the 5-min leadership task can help. It's not a classic management method but rather an attitude: "I consciously take 5 min for my team on a regular basis—not just in regular meetings, but in between. For a quick check-in, for attentive questions, for genuine interest."

Visibility of managers is particularly important during transformation. This doesn't just mean "being there"—it means "being approachable." Why? For many people, uncertainty goes hand in hand with reticence, and not everyone feels comfortable asking questions out loud. It takes trust to open up, especially when emotions are involved, such as fear about your job, your role, or worries about what may be expected of you.

The 5-min leadership task is a straightforward way to open up these spaces of trust. If this tool is introduced as a common leadership measure in change processes, the first changes will quickly become noticeable in the teams.

4.4   Empathetic Leadership Is a Key Skill

Processes of change are emotional, intense, and sometimes chaotic. Anyone who has to lead in this dynamic environment needs more than just methods and structures. They need a "feel" for people. This is exactly where **empathetic leadership** comes in—one of the most important leadership styles in times of transformation. Leaders who act *empathetically* build trust, retain people, and provide guidance—especially when there's no clear plan. They become stabilizing anchors in times of change.

The Basics of Empathetic Leadership

- Listen before you decide.
- Understand before you evaluate.
- Accompany before steering directly.

This type of interaction doesn't come easily to every manager—especially in situations of change, where quick and clear decisions are often crucial.

But many managers simply don't know **where to start.** How to show closeness without coming across as "soft." How to listen without immediately offering solutions. How to show presence—even when you yourself are unsure. In our experience, empathy is a skill that can be developed, for example through:

- **Active listening**: With genuine interest instead of a solution in mind.
- **Paying attention to what's left unsaid**: Body language, nuances, withdrawal.
- **Taking emotions seriously**: Even if you don't always understand them.

- **Showing yourself**: Not perfect, but human.
- **Putting relationships before results**: Or at least alongside them.

How Empathy Becomes Leadership Strength
HR and internal communications are the perfect team when it comes to enabling—and demanding—empathetic leadership. How HR and communications can support you:

- **Training and coaching**: Individual and confidential.
- **Peer formats**: Collegial exchange on current leadership topics.
- **Feedback rooms**: Looking back instead of retreating.
- **Impulses for new leadership roles**: For example, through communications teams, sparring, mentoring.
- **Use storytelling** to highlight positive examples of empathetic leadership.
- **Establish formats** in which managers can themselves experience, try things out, and grow—without losing face.

4.5   Identifying and Involving Multipliers

Every company has people who have a lot of informal influence. These don't have to be managers; they may be colleagues who have been with the company for a long time or who have earned special trust in other projects and situations and therefore help shape the culture and mood in the team today. It's important to identify them as part of the stakeholder analysis at the beginning of a change project and to seek dialogue with them.

If they're involved in the change at an early stage, they can act as multipliers and reinforce changes in a positive way. If they're ignored, there's a risk that they could undermine the change.

Leadership also means understanding networks and working with them consciously.

4.6 Takeaways

Good leadership in change processes means embracing change, listening to teams, communicating clearly, looking ahead, and addressing resistance. Those who remain in daily dialogue with the team recognize problems earlier and can anticipate what's coming. Managers translate strategy into everyday life and see resistance not as a disruption but as a signpost. They specifically involve informal opinion leaders to maintain momentum and direction. And they know that change always strikes at the heart—empathetic leaders provide support. Even brief "check-ins" can serve as anchors for trust and clarity.

1. Leadership in change processes requires clear communication, strategic foresight, and empathetic listening.
2. Change is always an emotional challenge. Leaders with empathy and openness create an environment that encourages change.
3. Good leadership in everyday life: brief check-ins are powerful levers for trust and clarity.

5

Communication as the Foundation of Change

Three key points:

1. **The secret ingredient of successful change is communication:**
   The best change strategy will be useless if people don't feel heard or included and start to resist. The combination of appropriate leadership and communication determines whether change succeeds or fails.
2. **Change requires more than just selective information—it needs continuity and trust:**
   Employees only accept change if it makes sense, allows participation, and takes place on an equal footing. Trust isn't built by timely announcements alone but through genuine dialogue.
3. **Change processes require not only results-oriented communication but also process communication:**
   It's important to define milestones and communicate what has been achieved. However, changes only become tangible and noticeable when the entire process is accompanied by communication.

A. Montua, *Guiding Transformation*, Business Guides on the Go, https://doi.org/10.1007/978-3-658-49755-2_5

These observations aren't just theoretical principles—addressing them in practice determines whether change succeeds or fails. Let's take a look at the challenges that arise when employees don't understand what's happening and what's expected of them. And how communication can help reduce resistance or prevent it from arising in the first place.

> **Example**
>
> David L. has been working as a production manager in a medium-sized technology company for 5 years. The organization is facing a major change: in order to remain internationally competitive, production is to be converted to agile manufacturing processes. This means shorter decision-making paths, more personal responsibility in the teams, and the use of new digital control systems.
>
> The strategy is in place, the technology is ready—but implementation is stalling. Resistance is palpable:
>
> - Many employees are afraid that their experience will be less valued because processes are being automated.
> - Managers feel bypassed because decisions are to be made in a more decentralized way in future.
> - Rumors about job cuts and crisis scenarios are circulating among the teams, and uncertainty is growing.
>
> David realizes that without a smart communication strategy that analyzes needs and tailors measures to the various target groups, this change won't succeed.

5.1 The Triad of Successful Change Communication

It's the most delicate phase of any transformation: change is palpable, but facts are lacking. This gray area determines whether trust will develop, or uncertainty will prevail.

Those who remain silent in the early stages of a transformation lose the power to interpret events. Employees expect guidance at this point—not general statements, but continuous insights into the state of affairs. Even if not everything has been decided yet, a clear message such as "We'll keep you informed" accompanied by regular updates (process communication) is more effective than any well-meaning "radio silence" and waiting until final decisions can be communicated (results communication).

We recommend a continuous triad of

- Information-giving
- Addressing emotional issues
- Empowerment

In the change process, it's not only the information itself that helps ("We're using new software"), but also the empowerment to implement it ("We're organizing workshops for everyone who works with it") and addressing the topic on an emotional level ("Here's a photo of our planning meeting—looking forward to great experiences using the software").

Important

Communication is especially important when there seems to be nothing to say. We all yawn now when we hear philosopher Paul Watzlawick's oft-quoted words: "You cannot not communicate." Nevertheless, his statement is one of the most important of all in situations of change. Because if we don't communicate, the vacuum is filled with all kinds of undesirable developments, such as rumors, fears, baggage, and the unchallenged assertions of others.

5.2 Persistence Pays off: Why Communicating Processes and Results Is So Important

There's no rule of thumb for the right amount of communication. However, one thing's certain: employees usually perceive anything that contains a disproportionate amount of content from just one of the three segments presented in the last section (information, emotionalization, and empowerment) as too much or too little information. That might mean, for example, constant communication at the information level without including emotional elements or the parts that make us feel empowered for what is to come.

If all segments are in balance, phases with particularly high or low information density can be better balanced and the topics can be communicated in a way that's easy to understand—and no one feels forgotten or overwhelmed.

It Pays to Stick with it: Process Communication in Everyday Life

Many change processes start gaining a lot of attention—and then lose visibility along the way. The energy from the kick-off fizzles out, none of the current projects has much news to report, and the grapevine is often the only source of information during these phases.

Yet it's precisely these intermediate phases that are crucial for motivation and connectivity. If people don't know whether and how things are progressing, their commitment declines—or they drop out internally. Process communication helps to prevent this by reporting continuously and honestly on where we stand—even when things come to a standstill.

Good process communication…

- … Provides orientation in times of uncertainty.
- … Shows that even small steps forward are valuable.
- … Engages people before they turn away.
- … Enables questions, discussion, and corrections.
- … Is transparent—even about conflicting goals, delays, or new insights.

Authentic insights that provide an overview and describe what's currently being worked on, what may already have been achieved, and how the journey will continue are helpful. This can take the form of short video statements, employee podcasts, interactive status boards, or storytelling formats such as "Behind the Change."

Every transformation has its dry spells. Times when decisions are still pending, pilot projects are underway, or results are unclear. That's precisely when communication is essential. Not to deliver content, but to create closeness. People want to know: *Are we still on track? Am I being seen? Is my contribution relevant? And they're grateful for honest answers, which could be, for example:* "We're still in the middle of it—and we're pursuing this path together."

Celebrate Successes: With Results Communication
Once the first results are visible, a second communication task begins: **identifying and reinforcing successes.** After all, what's communicated is perceived—and what's perceived becomes the norm.

Communicating results isn't self-congratulation, but rather reinforcement and consolidation. It shows:

- What we've achieved.
- Who made it possible.
- What follows from this—for all of us.

5.3 What to Do when Employees No Longer Believe in the Organization

A recurring difficulty in change processes: managers announce a new strategy—but skepticism spreads directly and simultaneously within the teams. "We've tried that before," "They can inform us a lot. Let's just wait it out," or "That's not going to work." These and similar reactions are typical signs of the state of credibility and trust among employees in the organization and the change processes which affect them.**How can this problem be solved? Four factors are crucial:**

1. **Change and transformation require credible stories**:
   Changes must be explained in a comprehensible and consistent manner. Why is this change necessary? Why now? What external or internal factors make it inevitable? What will happen if we don't change anything? And above all: What mistakes from the past have we recognized and will we avoid this time?
2. **Change is teamwork**:
   One-way communication ("This is how it's done") rarely leads to genuine acceptance. Managers and employees want to understand,

have a say, and exert influence. Space must be created for genuine exchange—and it's essential to allow critical questions and concerns to be raised.

3. **Change must be visible**:

    Nothing hurts change processes more than big announcements that aren't followed up by genuine action. If everything stays the same after the umpteenth "realignment," the workforce will lose trust for good. That's why it's important to make small changes/achieve small successes that are quickly visible and report on them to make the change tangible.

4. **Leadership shows the way**:

    Employees orient themselves to their immediate environment. Those who demand change must exemplify it themselves—through their own behavior, consistent decisions, and an authentic attitude.

Change Meets Resistance

Resistance during periods of change often seems like a disruptive factor, but it's actually valuable feedback. There are many reasons for this: fear of the unknown, the desire for familiarity, or the feeling of losing control. People who have worked according to fixed patterns for years can often perceive new requirements as a threat.

A lack of trust can also trigger resistance—in leadership, in the meaning of change, or in your own ability to keep up. This is often based on experience with failed projects. And sometimes it's about identity: when roles disappear, self-image falters.

Trust therefore becomes a key resource. The trust model (see Fig. 5.1, based on Frei/Morriss) describes three pillars that are needed to build and maintain trust: authenticity, logic, and empathy. Managers should be approachable, act in a comprehensible manner, and show genuine interest and connection. If one of these components is missing, trust suffers—and with it, the willingness to change.

When dealing with resistance, it's important to involve people in the change process. The issue is not how to break down resistance, but how to use it as a signal and steer it in a productive direction.

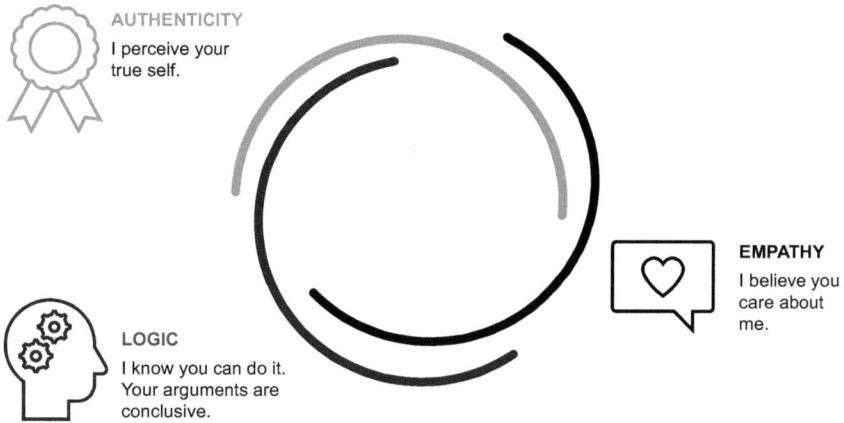

AUTHENTICITY
I perceive your
true self.

EMPATHY
I believe you
care about
me.

LOGIC
I know you can do it.
Your arguments are
conclusive.

Fig. 5.1 From "Begin with Trust," Frei & Morriss, 2020 (source: author's own representation)

5.4   Cognitive Biases in Change Communication

Why do people often understand messages differently than they were intended? Psychological effects play a major role here—and they influence how change processes are perceived. Managers and communication professionals should be aware of these distortions in order to convey messages effectively.

Common cognitive biases in the change process (including Nickerson, 1998; Baumeister et al., 2001; Felser, 2015; Eppler & Mengis, 2004; Samuelson & Zeckhauser, 1988; Tversky & Kahneman, 1974):

- **Confirmation bias**: People seek information that confirms their existing opinions and ignore contradictory facts. This reinforces their existing attitudes, making them more difficult to change.
- **Negativity bias**: Bad news sticks in our minds more than positive news. Change is often perceived as a threat, even if it brings long-term benefits.

- **Status quo bias**: People prefer what they're familiar with and often view change as a risk. Even rational arguments for change are therefore often met with resistance.
- **Anchor effect**: The first piece of information people receive on a topic acts as an anchor and influences all subsequent assessments. Early communication is therefore essential.
- **Framing effect**: The way a message is formulated influences its impact. The same information can generate confidence or fear depending on the choice of words.
- **Overload effect**: Too much information at once leads to overload and rejection. It's better to communicate in small chunks and use repetition in different media and formats in a targeted way.

What Does this Mean for Change Communication?

Those who are familiar with these mechanisms can formulate change messages in a more targeted manner and avoid misunderstandings. Here are some proven approaches:

- **Create positive narratives**: Communicate challenges not as threats, but as opportunities.
- **Set the tone early on**: Whoever shapes the first impression—that is, the basic narrative—lays the foundation for how change is perceived.
- **Use emotions in a targeted way**: A balance between factual arguments and emotional appeal ensures greater acceptance.
- **Provide information in doses**: Less is sometimes more. Clear core messages help to avoid overwhelming people.
- **Communicate in a way that's appropriate for the target group**: Different target groups have different fears and expectations—and need individually tailored communication.

5.5   The Right Channel for the Right Message

Not all communication is the same. For instance, the appropriate channel determines whether a message gets across—or fizzles out. But in many companies, the default solution is too often used: e-mail as an all-purpose tool, the "town hall" as a big stage with messages aimed at everyone. But what message calls for which framework? Which sender should deliver what message? And does the format even suit the sender?

A close look at the occasion, the format, and above all the sender can determine the success or failure of communication.

E-mail: Fast but Distant

- Ideal for facts, dates, and broad information. Not suitable for emotional messages.
- Suitable for: fact-based information.
- Advantages: fast, efficient, documentable.
- Skills: clear language, structure.

Town Hall Meetings: A Stage with Participation

- Good for relevant messages—but only really effective with interaction.
- Suitable for: strategic communication.
- Advantages: proximity, transparency, dialogue.
- Skills: openness, empathy.

Podcasts and Video Messages: Approachable from a Distance

- Strong impact on emotional topics—attitudes become visible.
- Suitable for: emotional communication.
- Advantages: authenticity, directness.
- Skills: naturalness, enthusiasm.

Executive Formats: Proximity at Eye Level

- Walk & talks, lunches, or breakfasts—informal and confidence-building.
- Suitable for: direct exchange.
- Advantages: dialogue, trust.
- Skills: genuine interest, listening.

CEO Blogs and Newsletters: Clear Language with Attitude

- Strategic topics summarized in writing.
- Suitable for: positioning, context.
- Advantages: consistency, depth.
- Skills: writing, clarity.

One-on-One   Conversations: Personal   Contact   Has   the Strongest Impact

- Individual concerns and resistance can be clarified in direct dialogue.
- Suitable for: team leadership.
- Advantages: trust, individuality.
- Skills: empathy, clarity.

Social Intranet and Chat Tools: Fast and Informal

- Good for updates and dialogue—not suitable for critical messages.
- Suitable for: everyday communication.
- Advantages: speed, networking.
- Skills: digital clarity, tact.

A single format will rarely suffice. Change only becomes tangible when information, attitudes, and dialogue work together—across channels and in line with the culture.

5.6   Dealing with Change Fatigue and Resistance

Change takes energy. Many organizations are currently experiencing change fatigue—a collective weariness with change. This is usually not caused by the change itself but by a perceived lack of direction, an absence of measurable success, and overload from too many parallel projects. When change becomes a never-ending task with no noticeable effect, the mood eventually shifts: commitment turns to resistance, interest becomes resignation.

In our experience, it's therefore worthwhile to regularly check the "energy levels" of an organization. The key question is: How is our system responding to change—and how can we counteract this in a targeted way through communication or leadership initiatives (see Fig. 5.2)?

The following energy states can prevail (Bruch & Vogel, 2009):

- **Positive energy**: Here, the energy for change is high and constructive. There's a spirit of optimism, teams think for themselves and actively drive things forward.
- **Corrosive energy**: Here, too, there is a lot of energy in the system—but in a negative direction. Things are simmering, resistance is forming, criticism is becoming vocal. Sounds unpleasant, but it's a workable state—because the energy's there.
- **Comfortable inertia**: Sounds good at first, but it's tricky. Everything runs smoothly, there is no open rejection—but also no drive. A typical state in companies that "have already achieved so much."

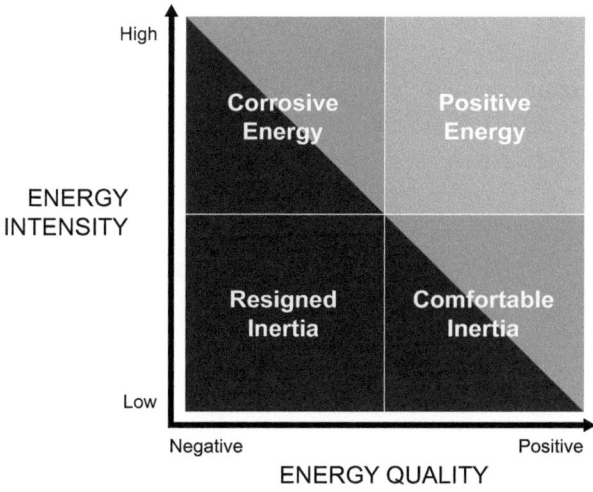

Fig. 5.2 Based on "States of Organizational Energy," Bruch, H. & Vogel, B. (source: author's own representation)

- **Resigned inertia**: The most dangerous state. There's neither drive nor conflict, only withdrawal, passivity, and inner resignation.

Project teams, communication managers, and executives can use this scheme to assess where they currently stand. And above all: How can we generate positive energy in a targeted way—or maintain it? These key questions will help:

1. What's the urgency for change?
2. Why is it worth the effort?
3. What happens if we do nothing?

How Can you Tell if Change Fatigue Has Reached a Critical Level?
A quiet withdrawal is often one of the first warning signs. Employees continue to do their jobs, but they no longer show any enthusiasm and only do what's absolutely necessary. Sometimes this manifests itself in ironic comments, sometimes in declining participation in meetings, or in an increasing number of sick days.

Managers and communicators should recognize such signals early on and take countermeasures. Psychological safety plays a key role here. Employees should feel that they can express their concerns without fear of negative consequences. Open spaces for honest conversations are needed—not only in the form of traditional feedback rounds, but also in direct exchanges between managers and teams.

5.7 The "Golden Circle" as a Guardrail along the Way

Especially in phases of exhaustion or resistance, clear communication that makes sense and generates emotional resonance is needed. But even in the initial communication of a change process, it helps to clearly and concisely communicate the reasons why: Why are we changing now and not before or later? Why in the direction that has now been set? And why does what we are planning make sense right now?

Simon Sinek's well-known "Golden Circle" model (Sinek, 2009) offers a helpful structure for this. It consists of three rings: Why, How, and What—looked at from the inside out. At the core is the Why: Why are we doing what we're doing? This is followed by the How: How are we implementing it? And on the outside is the What: What exactly are we doing? Sinek turns the usual way of thinking on its head—don't think in terms of the product, but in terms of the meaning.

In a transformation, the model helps to create clarity, because knowing the why provides orientation and connects people emotionally. The how translates the meaning into principles and actions. And the what shows what happens in specific terms. This creates a common thread—from the inside out.

5.8 Winning Employees as Change Ambassadors

People orient themselves toward other people—not toward company presentations. If you really want to bring change into your organization and make a difference, you need multipliers. But not every colleague is equally suited to communicating messages of change. It's crucial to involve the right people in a targeted way and to support them effectively.

How do you win employees as change ambassadors?

- **Voluntary participation instead of obligation**: Employees should be intrinsically motivated. Those who are truly convinced can also convince others.
- **Appreciation and involvement**: People who are involved in the change process in their everyday work, and are asked for their opinions when decisions are made, feel heard and are more committed.
- **Training and support**: Change ambassadors need clear information to be able to communicate confidently.
- **Clear roles and expectations**: What exactly does it mean to be a change ambassador? Defining tasks and responsibilities from the outset helps to avoid uncertainty.

- **Regular exchange**: A network needs platforms for exchange, feedback, and continuous development.
- **Consider the time required for change work**: Being a change ambassador should not require overtime. Colleagues need at least 10–20% of their regular working time for these important tasks. This should also be communicated to the team.

An effective strategy is to specifically involve informal opinion leaders in the change process. Thanks to their credibility and proximity to the teams, they can drive change in a completely different way than official communication channels are able to. This turns a loose group of multipliers into a strategically managed, effective network.

5.9 Communicating Quick Wins and Initial Successes

Intermediate stages are important milestones on the long road to transformation. These pauses and recovery phases are necessary to look back at what has already been achieved, celebrate successes, perhaps make a few adjustments, check our mood, and keep everyone's motivation as high as possible.

Quick wins—that is, visible successes which are communicated—are important because they:

- … Build trust: employees see that things are really happening and that it's worthwhile to be part of the journey.
- … Make change tangible: overarching strategic goals often seem abstract. Small successes show how change is being implemented in everyday life.
- … Motivate: experiences of success fuel long-term willingness to change.

It's crucial that these successes are made visible in a targeted way, otherwise they won't have the desired effect. This can be done through a short "success" video, an internal message, a small milestone celebration, or recognition by management in town hall meetings or with tailored gestures.

5.10 Rituals and Symbols to Anchor the Transformation

Change doesn't just happen in processes and structures but also in the minds and hearts of employees. Rituals and symbolic actions help move change from the factual to the emotional level. **Examples of rituals in the change process:**

- **Kick-off events for new change or transformation phases**: The conscious starting point of a change, where the "why" and "where to" are made tangible—and even entertaining.
- **Milestone celebrations**: Celebrating progress together.
- **Visual changes**: New workspace designs, changed working environments, or symbols of change.
- **Joint reflection sessions**: Regular check-ins to gauge the mood and make adjustments.

Such rituals strengthen the sense of community, keep the willingness to change in focus, and make the transformation tangible. **Rituals that can be actively shaped by employees are particularly effective.**

5.11 Takeaways

Change begins in the mind and in the heart—and communication carries us through the joint process. In a world where organizations are constantly changing, it isn't only the quality of the strategy that determines success but primarily whether it's possible to get people on board.

- **Communication is the critical factor for success in phases of change:** It determines the acceptance, speed, and depth of the change.
- **Communication needs rhythm:** The frequency must be appropriate to the phase, topic, and target group.
- **A change process doesn't end with the final workshop:** Rituals, symbols, and storytelling help to anchor change permanently.

References

Baumeister, R. F., Bratslavsky, E., Finkenauer, C., & Vohs, K. D. (2001). Bad is stronger than good. *Review of General Psychology, 5*(4), 323–370.

Bruch, H., & Vogel, B. (2009). *Organizational energy: Bringing companies to high voltage.* Gabler Verlag.

Frei, F., & Morriss, A. (2020, May–June). *Begin with trust. Harvard Business Review.* [See also: https://hbr.org/2020/05/begin-with-trust].

Felser, G. (2015). *Advertising and consumer psychology* (4th ed.).

Eppler, M. J., & Mengis, J. (2004). The concept of information overload: A review of literature from organization science, accounting, marketing, MIS, and related disciplines. *The Information Society, 20*(5), 325–344.

Nickerson, R. S. (1998). Confirmation bias: A ubiquitous phenomenon in many guises. *Review of General Psychology, 2*(2), 175–220.

Samuelson, W., & Zeckhauser, R. (1988). Status quo bias in decision making. *Journal of Risk and Uncertainty, 1*(1), 7–59.

Sinek, S. (2009). *Start with why: How great leaders inspire everyone to take action.* Portfolio/Penguin.

Tversky, A., & Kahneman, D. (1974). Judgment under uncertainty: Heuristics and biases. *Science, 185*(4157), 1124–1131.

6

Heroes Around the Campfire: Stories of Transformation

Three key points:

1. **Stories and a "big picture" are important and effective supports in change processes**:
   They emotionalize, simplify, and provide orientation.
2. **A suitable change story makes change comprehensible and emotive**:
   Thinking them through and using them from the outset channels energy and anchors messages.
3. **Negative narratives can subconsciously block change**:
   Recognizing and reinterpreting these is a decisive factor for success.

Without a strong narrative, change remains abstract, difficult to grasp, and often hard to feel and understand. Stories are vehicles that help embed change emotionally and make it understandable, allowing us to find our way into the hearts, minds, and routines of our employees.

But how does this work in practice? What challenges arise when companies try to tell their change story? And how can managers use narratives in a targeted way to win employees over to change?

Example

An international logistics company is facing profound changes. The industry is transforming rapidly: automation, artificial intelligence, and new market requirements call for a radical rethink. But the image that dominates within the company is: "We're a solid, heavyweight organization—innovation and agility are for start-ups, not for us."
This perception leads to noticeable challenges:

1. Employees feel at home in the old world and don't believe that their company needs innovation.
2. Managers are unsure whether they can credibly communicate the need for a transformation.
3. The reactions to internal communication formats reflect this skepticism: initiatives for change are met with resistance because the narrative that has developed over time is deeply entrenched.

Sarah L., head of internal communications, recognizes the challenge: Change itself isn't enough—the company needs a new story. One that isn't based on deficits but on strengths. One that picks up on the firm's long tradition and history, turns it into something positive, and derives strengths for the future from it. Together with her team, she sets to work.

6.1 The Big Picture

Complex transformations often put companies in a paradoxical situation: on paper, projects are running smoothly, the necessary steps are being taken as part of a new strategy, and the management has given the green light. At the same time, however, the majority of the workforce lacks a clear vision of the bigger picture, with workers asking themselves: "Why are we doing all this? So many individual projects, each of which is causing unrest. Where is this going?" Not to mention the lack of commitment and support for the transformation that is so urgently needed. Uncertainty of this kind often leads to change processes stalling, resistance that hinders progress, and motivation being lost.

If we want to make transformation a success, we need clear goals and a shared understanding of the overall transformation—a big picture that tidies up the loose ends and explains how everything fits together. Without a clear and shared understanding of the change, employees quickly feel disoriented, even if they are actually committed and motivated. The roles of the big picture:

- **Ensure understanding**: If an idea is to be supported and promoted, it must be understood.
- **Make effective use of synergies**: Employees need an explanation of the meaning and purpose of their tasks within the overall structure of the transformation.
- **Focus on the big picture**: Especially in times of change, we seek orientation and security. If we're given the opportunity to understand the big picture and the meaning behind the individual steps, we're more willing to invest our energy in the process.

Once the big picture has been successfully communicated, people in the company should be able to answer the following questions:

- What's the main goal we're aiming for with the changes?
- What individual steps will we take to get there?
- How do my tasks and activities relate to this goal?
- What's expected of me in this change?

This allows us to tie up loose ends and create a strong, resilient rope that connects everything together!

6.2 How Stories Support Change

Similar to change and transformation, the terms "change story" and "narrative" are often used interchangeably. However, it's important to define them more clearly so that companies can then decide more effectively what's needed:

- A **narrative** is an overarching thought pattern or fundamental assumption about reality that spans many stories and shapes the culture of an organization or the perceptions of the people who work in it. It's deeply embedded in an organization's culture and influences how people interpret change.
- A **change story** is a deliberately told story within a change process that either confirms or challenges the existing narrative. Its goal is to make change understandable, stir emotions, and win people over to a new direction. While narratives have a long-term effect and are often unconscious, change stories are consciously used communication tools to actively shape transformation.

People love stories. They're embedded in our DNA and help us process information.

Stories of change, known as change stories, reduce complexity by highlighting patterns, appealing to emotions, and situating change in a comprehensible context. A well-told change story makes the future tangible and makes it easier for those involved to identify with the change. Without a strong narrative, change remains abstract—with a good story, it becomes a shared adventure.

Stories have the power to move people and influence their behavior. Studies suggest that information embedded in a story is remembered much better than pure facts. Why? Because stories activate our brains—not only the areas that process language, but also those responsible for emotions and empathy. Powerful change stories therefore work not just on a cognitive level but on an emotional one. And that's precisely what makes them such effective tools.

So if the basic assumption about reality—in other words, the narrative—is "We're too slow for innovation," then the change story would have to challenge this narrative in order to change it in people's minds.

Overall narratives are part of the culture, and individual stories are the building blocks for changing them. If the entire narrative is to be changed, several stories are needed in the long term.

A company that perceives itself as "long-established but outdated" will find it difficult to innovate. A company that sees itself as a "pioneer that's always finding new ways" will find change easier. Therefore, if you want change, you need to understand the dominant narrative of the organization—and, if necessary, retell it.

A vivid example of this is the LEGO company. In the early 2000s, the Danish toy manufacturer fell into a serious crisis. The dominant narrative was: "We're a classic toy manufacturer." But this idea was no longer suited to an increasingly digital world. It was only when LEGO changed its narrative to "We're a creative platform for play, learning, and imagination" that the turnaround to an innovative and modern company began. LEGO became successful again (Robertson & Breen, 2013).

6.3 Recognizing and Changing Negative Narratives

Every organization unconsciously tells stories about itself. Unfortunately, these often hinder change processes. Anyone who hears statements such as "We're a cumbersome tanker" or "That will never work for us" is dealing with deeply rooted negative narratives. The trick is to reinterpret them.

Ask yourself:

- What statements about your own company do you hear repeatedly, in different areas and situations?
- Where is change portrayed as impossible?
- Which "We've always done it this way" statements dominate?
- What stories do managers and long-term employees tell about the company?
- In which situations do these narratives hinder solution-oriented thinking?
- What positive narratives already exist—and how can they be reinforced?

Why Are Obstructive Narratives So Persistent?
Behind these narratives are often cognitive biases that unconsciously influence our thinking and actions (see also Sect. 5.4):

- **Status quo bias:** "It has worked well so far, so it should stay that way." Change seems riskier than the familiar.
- **Negativity bias:** Negative experiences have a stronger impact on us than positive ones. A failed change project stays in our memory longer than ten successful ones.
- **Self-confirmation bias:** We unconsciously seek evidence that supports our existing view—and ignore counterexamples.

How Can Narratives Be Reinterpreted?

- **Think from problem to opportunity:**
  From "We're a cumbersome tanker" to "We're a stable rock in stormy times."
  From "Our processes are too slow" to "Our processes are thorough and well thought-out."
- **Think from resistance to strength:**
  From "That has never worked here" to "We prove that we can overcome challenges."
  From "Our employees are skeptical about change" to "Our employees ask critical questions and ensure well-founded decisions."
- **Think from the past to the future:**
  From "We're a traditional company" to "We combine tradition with innovation."
  From "We have a rigid hierarchy" to "Our clear structure provides orientation and reliability."

6.4   The Change Story Formula

Good change stories make change understandable and tangible. A clear and strong structure helps to engage listeners emotionally. A good way to do this is to tell heroic stories, known as "hero's journeys": Who's affected by which problem? And then where, and what aspects, do they change? Classic storytelling relies on five elements:

1. **Hero**: Who's experiencing the change? Who's affected or needs to take action? (e.g., a team, a manager, an entire organization).
2. **Problem**: What's the central dilemma? Why is change necessary? (e.g., market changes, inefficient processes, internal resistance).
3. **Turning point**: What changes the perspective on the problem? Is there a realization, external pressure, or a moment of clarity?
4. **Solution**: What specific steps will lead out of the crisis? What does the new path look like? (e.g., new strategies, measures, changes in attitude or structure).
5. **Impact**: What is the tangible result? How has the situation improved? What positive effects can be felt?

The stories don't have to be long. Sometimes five sentences are enough:

1. This is how it used to be: (initial situation).
2. Then this happened: (event that necessitated change).
3. We need to change: (realization and challenge).
4. So now we're doing this: (solution, measures).
5. Now our world looks like this: (success, positive conclusion).

> **Example**
>
> "Our company grew rapidly, but our processes were slow. Then a new competitor came along which could deliver twice as fast. We realized that we couldn't go on like this. So we streamlined our processes, made our teams more agile, and introduced new software. Since then, we have been faster and more efficient than ever before."

6.5 Using Stories as a Leadership Tool

Strong narratives also help managers shape change, inspire teams, reduce fears, and promote engagement. They should:

- Be clear and simple: reduce complexity to understandable messages.
- Be emotionally engaging: facts alone aren't convincing—but when combined with emotions, they are.

- Remain authentic: credibility is the key to trust.
- Paint a picture of the future: people follow visions, not action plans.

A great example of the power of change stories is Nasa's Apollo program. Instead of merely talking about technical challenges, John F. Kennedy managed to create a clear narrative in his famous Moon speech: "We choose to go to the Moon in this decade [...] not because it is easy, but because it is hard" (nasa.gov, 2022). This inspiring narrative united millions of people behind a common vision.

6.6   Takeaways

Change begins in people's minds—and often with stories about the new direction of their own company. If you want to shape change successfully, you shouldn't only devise strategies but also tell the right stories. Managers can use storytelling in a targeted way to provide orientation, strengthen motivation, and win people over to the change process.

- Change needs good stories—without them, change remains abstract.
- Successful change stories follow a clear structure (hero—problem—turning point—solution—impact).
- Reinterpreting negative narratives means turning obstacles into opportunities and the past into the future.

References

Kennedy, John F. (2022, September 7). *Presidential library and museum–Speech at Rice University.* nasa.gov, Accessed Apr 25, 2025, from https://www.nasa.gov/history/60-years-ago-president-kennedy-reaffirms-moon-landing-goal-in-rice-university-speech/ (The 10 most important leadership lessons I've learned)

Robertson, D., & Breen, B. (2013). *Brick by brick: How LEGO rewrote the rules of innovation and conquered the global toy industry.* Crown.

7

Return on Change: How Transformation Becomes Measurable

Three key points:

1. **Transformation can and should have an impact:**
   When organizations change, there is often a lot at stake—sometimes even their very existence. Success then becomes a management task. Change management and communication have key roles to play: they ensure that messages aren't just sent but also heard, understood, and internalized by the right people.
2. **"Soft" doesn't mean "vague":**
   Culture, trust, communication—all crucial "soft" factors for success. But they aren't black boxes. With the right methods, they become visible and controllable. Soft facts can be translated into intelligent metrics.
3. **Success begins with clear goals:**
   If you want to measure impact, you have to define it before you create it. It should be clear from the planning stage: What exactly do we want to change? And how will we know if we've succeeded?

© The Author(s), under exclusive license to Springer Fachmedien
Wiesbaden GmbH, part of Springer Nature 2025
A. Montua, *Guiding Transformation*, Business Guides on the Go,
https://doi.org/10.1007/978-3-658-49755-2_7

Change costs time, money, attention, and nerves. And it can often lead to uncertainty. That's another reason why it's so important to be able to show those involved that it's worth it. This journey has a destination. And yes, it's having an impact.

But what does "*impact*" actually mean? Transformation processes aren't just about what's visible—new structures, new tools, new processes. They're primarily about what people experience, understand, internalize, and what changes for them. This is why measurability is so challenging—and at the same time so crucial.

Impact isn't measured months later with hindsight—it's decided from the outset. Evaluations should therefore be considered right at the start of the change process.

Success Starts with Clear Goals

If we want to measure impact, we first need to clarify how we define it. Even during the planning phase of a change project, one question should therefore be at the top of the agenda: *What does success look like?*

Without this clarity of objectives, any evaluation remains vague. For instance, we might assess the number of clicks on the intranet and call it "reach"—without knowing whether anyone really understood what it was all about. Or we count workshop participants without knowing what they individually took away from their experiences.

"Soft" Isn't "Vague"

One of the most common excuses when it comes to evaluation is: *"That can't be measured."* This usually refers to cultural factors: attitude, trust, psychological safety. All aspects that are often dismissed as "soft topics." But soft doesn't mean invisible, or even unimportant. On the contrary, it's precisely these factors that determine the success or failure of transformation processes.

With the right methodology, these areas can be systematically observed, described, and developed. Whether employees are getting involved, whether managers are seen as credible, whether a new culture is actually being lived—all of this can be measured. Not always in numbers, but always in feedback and impact.

Measure What Count—Not Just What's Easy to Count

In many companies, the focus is on measuring what's comparatively easy to quantify: How many e-mails were sent? How many visits and likes did an article receive? How many people attended the information event? For how many minutes was the video viewed, and by how many? All of this can be helpful, but it often only scratches the surface.

Because what we really want to know is something more:
Did it make a difference? Did our actions cause people to think differently, act differently, get involved in a more meaningful way, make decisions, or support our cause?
A helpful model for measuring impact therefore distinguishes between three levels:

- **Output**: What was done? What measures were implemented?
- **Outcome**: What has changed in behavior or attitude?
- **Impact**: What long-term contribution does the whole measure make to the corporate strategy?

It helps to think about impact holistically—and not just stop at counting measures.

Impact Measurement Requires a System—And a Story

If you want to make impact visible, you need an effective set-up: clear goals, appropriate indicators, reliable data. But numbers alone are only convincing when they're embedded in a story. In a context that makes it clear *why* something's important—and *where* the journey is headed.

It's also important to consider the target audience: an executive board needs different information than a team lead or a project manager. Managers might be interested in participation and attitudes within the team, while employees might be more interested in their opportunities for shaping the future and their influence. Good impact measurement takes all this into account and closely integrates communication and evaluation.

The combination of quantitative and qualitative data is particularly valuable: hard numbers meet soft signals. A mood barometer in the focus group can sometimes explain more than a five-digit click count.

Tell the Impact Story—Don't Just Report it

Measuring is good. Understanding is better. But making impact tangible is what really changes the game. Because change requires not only control but energy. And energy arises when people experience that something is happening. That their contributions count. That it makes a difference whether they get involved or not.

That's why impact measurement always includes an impact story. This can take many forms:

- A dynamic change dashboard on the intranet.
- Short video statements from managers.
- Or real stories of change from within the organization—honest, specific, and relatable.

Don't just show numbers. Show developments. And show that we're learning. We're listening. We're improving.

Takeaways

- Impact begins with clarity of purpose. Without it, change remains vague.
- Measuring success isn't just another control tool, but a management tool. It creates transparency, trust, and the ability to learn.
- Cultural and emotional issues are also tangible—with the right questions and methods.
- Good impact measurement thinks in terms of results—not channels.
- And above all: impact is felt when what's being done is seen, comprehended, and communicated.

8

Power and Micropolitics: The Underestimated Dimension in Transformation Processes

Three key points:

1. **Transformation is also a political process:**
   Those who focus solely on concepts and measures fail to recognize the dynamics of interests, loyalty, and power.
2. **Micropolitics isn't inherently bad—it's human:**
   Informal power struggles, "old boy networks," and blockades aren't necessarily disruptive but rather part of organizational reality.
3. **Leadership requires clarity—even in change processes and conflicts:**
   Those who want to shape transformation must be able to withstand tensions, balance interests, and be politically capable of acting.

Desire for (More) Influence

When organizations change, power relations usually shift as well. Old certainties are lost, new roles emerge, and previous routines are suddenly up for debate. And where power shifts, resistance arises—sometimes overtly, sometimes quietly.

© The Author(s), under exclusive license to Springer Fachmedien Wiesbaden GmbH, part of Springer Nature 2025
A. Montua, *Guiding Transformation*, Business Guides on the Go, https://doi.org/10.1007/978-3-658-49755-2_8

Many change initiatives therefore fail due to informal power issues: when key individuals lose motivation, when hidden coalitions form, or when informal leaders undermine agendas. This is often done not out of malice but because every change affects interests. And because power is rarely relinquished voluntarily.

Those who ignore this will be overtaken by reality. Those who recognize it can shape change more realistically—and more successfully.

Micropolitics Is Organization in Action

In every organization, at least two "realities" exist side by side:

- The **formal world** with processes, roles, and decision-making paths.
- The **informal world** with networks, spheres of influence, and unspoken (power) rules.

In change projects, the informal side often becomes the secret decision-making arena. This is because it helps determine who is heard—and who isn't. Whose opinion counts, even if it's not on paper. And what ideas survive—and which ones don't.

Micropolitics isn't a "dirty game" but a survival strategy in complex systems. People secure influence, protect their turf, and position themselves for the future. This isn't always pleasant—but it's everyday life and lived reality.

Power Shifts Often Mean Identity Shifts

When power is challenged, identity is often shaken as well. Those who have been regarded as decision-makers, spokespeople, or experts for years often experience transformation not as a technical process, but as a personal turning point.

Change can trigger hurt feelings—and powerlessness. Many micropolitical reactions are therefore not tactically motivated, but emotional: shame, fear of losing control, the feeling of no longer being needed.

Experienced managers in particular sometimes interpret new structures as a creeping loss of power. Leadership here means perceiving tensions, interpreting dynamics, and creating spaces in which these emotions can be processed. Without shaming anyone.

The Blind Spot of Communication

The topic of power is often left out of official messaging around change. Instead there's often talk of visions, milestones, and "joint paths." That sounds good—but it fails to recognize that transformation usually also produces losers. Even if it's only in people's own minds. Those who lose influence don't need platitudes but honest assessment.

Communication that ignores issues of power only makes power more effective—in the shadows and underground. Credible communication about change therefore identifies what's at stake: Who gets more freedom to shape the future? Who gets less? Which decisions are being shifted—and why?

Not all answers have to be on the table immediately and from the outset. But the questions shouldn't just disappear.

Power Is Also Evident in Symbols

Who speaks first in a meeting? Who sits at the front of the town hall—and who sits at the back? Who is allowed to disagree without risking anything?

Power is often evident not only in structures but also in symbols. Rituals, language, seating arrangements, dress codes—all of these convey subconsciously who's actually in charge.

This symbolic level should also be addressed: open meetings to all areas of the company, create new formats, give space to perspectives that otherwise might not be heard. Small gestures—big impact.

In a manufacturing company, a new division manager takes responsibility for an agile restructuring. He brings fresh ideas with him—and encounters invisible walls. The team leaders nod in workshops, but remain stuck in their old structures. Decisions are put on hold, pilot projects are blocked, and information is only passed on selectively.

The official communication sounds like a new beginning—the reality is more like cold resistance.

Only after talking to key people does it become clear that many feel overlooked and fear for their influence. The division manager responds: instead of introducing even more changes, he starts listening. He redistributes responsibility, openly addresses fears, and creates small successes. The dynamic shifts—slowly but noticeably.

Typical Micropolitical Patterns in Transformation

- "Yes [with a tacit 'but...']":
- Seemingly open agreement accompanied by silent obstruction—for example, through delay or failure to implement new measures.
- Coalitions of the insecure:
- Managers and employees join forces—not from principle but out of fear of losing power.
- Symbolic obedience:
- "We're agile now" or "We have OKRs too"—but the old patterns in approvals and processes live on.
- Loyalty dilemmas:
- Managers are caught between the expectations of the company and those of their teams.
- Securing positions through sabotage:
- Individuals subtly block progress—for example, through selective communication or exaggerated analyses of the risks.

What leadership can do

1. **Make dynamics visible**:
   Sociograms, stakeholder mappings, tension analyses—use tools that help you understand informal realities.

2. **Create space for genuine conversations**:

   What can't be said? Who feels threatened—or overlooked? Transformation requires protected spaces for honest discourse.

3. **Remain politically capable of acting**:

   Leadership also means enduring discussions and tensions, moderating interests—and staying on course at the same time.

4. **Build coalitions of enablement**:

   Change can't be achieved alone. It requires allies who enjoy trust and can bring informal power to bear.

Those who lead through transformation aren't only faced with strategic tasks, they're also right in the middle of a political playing field. And that's a good thing. Because organizations don't change in a vacuum, but through people—with all their interests, fears, and stories.

A smart leader recognizes this. They hear what *isn't* being said. They understand that resistance is often a signal. They decide when to moderate—and when to decide. And they know that those who don't fear micropolitics, but shape it, gain more than power. They win trust.

Takeaways

- Transformation also changes power relationships—and that creates friction.
- Micropolitics is part of every organization—it shouldn't be suppressed but taken on board and discussed.
- Those who recognize and address tensions create clarity and the ability to act.
- Leadership in transformation also means moderating between interests, forming alliances, and tolerating contradictions.
- Taking an honest look at informal dynamics is often the turning point in the change process.

9

Concluding Remarks

Transformation isn't a fixed state but a mixture of the right strategy, leaders who enable and live change, and a tailored communicating of processes and results.

Change is therefore not a project with a start and end date. It isn't a single item on a to-do list, it's a state of movement—sometimes quiet, sometimes lively, sometimes joyful, and sometimes uncomfortable.

My hope is that this book will provide you, dear reader, with ideas that will help you shape this dynamic—with clarity, conviction, and the belief that real change begins with people. Whether you provide guidance as a manager, *translate change processes into everyday life* as a communicator, provide support *as an HR manager,* or steer overall projects as an organizational developer and change professional: your role is crucial.

Perhaps you've even recognized yourself in one or two places. Maybe you've discovered a new tool, questioned an old way of thinking, or found new stories that you'd like to tell in the future. I would be delighted—because nothing's more powerful than a brilliant idea, a perfectly timed suggestion, or the ideal hero's journey at just the right moment.

Are you interested in learning more about practical applications? On our **landing page**, you'll find additional materials, including **checklists, best practices, in-depth articles, and audio clips**. Everything is concise, clear, and immediately applicable, just like this book. https://montua-partner.de/essentials

Thank you for following our thoughts and ideas this far. I wish you courage, clarity, and many good conversations as you navigate what will hopefully be a successful next change. And if you'd like to exchange ideas, I look forward to hearing from you—at buch@montuapartner.de.

Best Regards,

Andrea Montua.

Essentials You'll Take Away from this

- **Make transformation tangible instead of managing change**: You'll learn the difference between change and real transformation – experience culture, attitudes, and communication as the decisive levers for sustainable change.
- **Help shape the future instead of just watching it unfold**: You'll learn how motivation, psychological safety, and authentic storytelling can turn employees into co-creators instead of mere bystanders.
- **Recognize communication as a factor for success**: You'll read about the tools, suggestions for action, and dialogue formats that managers, HR, and communication professionals need to make change happen, convince people, and bring new ideas to life.